FOLLOWING THE FISHING

David Butcher

The days when bands of Scots fisher girls followed the herring fleets round Britain and scores of trades depended on the harvest of the sea

1

AT THE FISHING GROUNDS.

Published 1987 by

Tops'l Books
(an imprint of David & Charles)
Newton Abbot London North Pomfret (Vt)

British Library Cataloguing in Publication Data

Butcher, David, *1942–*
Following the fishing : the days when bands of Scots fisher girls followed the herring fleets round Britain....
1. Fishers—Great Britain—Social life and customs
I. Title
941 HD8039.F66G7

ISBN 0-7153-9108-9

Printed in Great Britain
by Redwood Burn Ltd, Trowbridge, Wilts
for David & Charles Publishers plc
Brunel House Newton Abbot Devon

The text of this book contains many specialised local, technical and nautical words which may not be familiar to the general reader. To avoid peppering the pages with footnotes and explanations a full glossary is included at the back.

Also in this series
The Driftermen
The Trawlermen
Living From The Sea

Front cover. Itinerant Scottish fisher girls at work on The Denes at Lowestoft.

A cooper making a barrel some eighty years ago. The staves were thoroughly wetted. It was the combination of dampness and the effect of heat from a brazier-held fire within the barrel itself, which enabled the characteristic shape to be achieved.

Contents

Chapter		Page
	Preface	6
	The Folk Who Told The Tale	8
1.	Scotch Cure	11
2.	The Klondyke Trade	21
3.	Trading In Herrings	32
4.	Gone West	39
5.	Selling The Catches	45
6.	Salt And Smoke	55
7.	Factory Processes	63
8.	Boxes And Tins	69
9.	The Ice Factory	74
10.	Net Making And Mending	79
11.	Baskets Galore	86
12.	Building Drifters	93
13.	Triple Expansion	103
14.	Railway Days	110
—	Conclusion	117
—	Glossary	119
—	Bibliography	125

Preface

When the British fishing industry was at its zenith it was reckoned that every steam drifter that went to sea provided a hundred jobs ashore. How accurate that figure was is now impossible to check, but it will not be very far out and gives some indication of the importance of fishing to the economy in the earlier part of this century. In many parts fishing was of course the major employer on which practically the whole local community depended.

This book is the fourth I have devoted to recording the oral history of the East Anglian fishing industry in the first half of this century. The first two dealt with life at sea in the two main "disciplines" of fishing, drifting and trawling, and the third with the shoreside and social life of the communities involved. This volume records the life and work of that great army of shoreworkers, men and women, whose skills kept the fishing fleets sailing – and whose livelihood in turn depended on the ships at sea.

Those skills were many and varied, for fishing was (and still is today, even in its reduced form) a labour-intensive industry. During the first half of this century the numbers of shore personnel involved in the ancillary industries may have numbered as many as a million nation wide, with women being especially important in the making and mending of nets and in the processing of herrings. There was a good deal of migratory labour involved as well, with Lowestoft and Yarmouth people travelling to the West Country, to Scotland and to the Shetlands, and with the annual influx into East Anglia every autumn of folk from north of the border, particularly the hardy herring girls, details of whose life have been little recorded previously. It was movement which enriched the respective areas involved (enriched in every sense of the word) and even though the population shifts ended some time ago, the links forged between communities have still not entirely ceased to exist.

As far as Great Yarmouth and Lowestoft are concerned, fishing and the allied trades were of paramount importance. This was especially true of the latter town, which did not have as large and diverse a maritime trade as its neighbour, nor so considerable a number of holidaymakers during the summer months. Yarmouth also had a wider industrial base, as it would be termed today, whereas Lowestoft (with the exception of a factory that built bus bodies) was almost entirely geared to fishing and associated trades. An idea of the closeness of community which existed in fishing ports is reflected by the sundry cross-references of person, place and fact throughout the text of this book. These were not deliberately sought from my respondents, but occurred quite naturally as I gathered the information.

Obviously, I owe a great deal to the people who helped me by agreeing to be recorded and to those folk who introduced me to them. A number of the tapes used here are among the first ones I ever did, back in the spring and summer of 1976, which makes it inevitable that some contributors (given their ages) are no longer with us. Thus their evidence about the age in which they lived is all the more valuable. The book should stand as a fitting tribute to them and the generation they represented.

With regard to the illustrations I am grateful once more to my colleague, Rick Turrell, who took most of the portraits. Jack Rose has, as always, been most generous in providing pictures from his large collection and given encouragement to me in my researches. Captain S. T. Smith of Scarborough, Editor of Olsen's Fisherman's Nautical Almanack has also once again been most helpful.

As before, I have left the people telling the story speak for themselves with the minimum of interpolation. After all, it was their experience and their words can bring those now vanished days to life for the reader better than any writer or historian could hope to do.

Inevitably, all these specialised occupations have their own vocabulary, often incomprehensible to outsiders. For this reason a glossary has been included at the end and where it has been thought helpful difficult words have been shown in italic where they first appear to remind you to turn to the glossary.

The Folk Who Told The Tale

ERNIE ARMES (born 1902) – spent the whole of his working life in the fish trade, being based on the Lowestoft market for much of the time. Between the wars he was employed by German herring export companies and travelled the coasts to buy for them.

STANLEY BIRD (born 1917) – entered the family basket-making business at an early age and has been connected with it ever since. The demise of the Yarmouth fishing industry has now caused his firm to seek other markets.

FRANK BRISTOW (born 1913) – the son of a traditional smoker with one of the big Yarmouth fish-curing companies. He started work in the processing industry himself with a firm that produced fish pastes and became manager of one of the early deep freezing plants in Lowestoft.

ARTHUR COLLINS (born 1914) – spent his working life before the war with a timber firm which produced the wide range of fish-boxes required to keep the industry going.

ARTHUR EVANS (1901–1984) – the son of a leading Lowestoft fish merchant who followed in father's footsteps.

MARY FISK (born 1896) – member of a Pakefield fishing family who, like so many girls of her generation, learned the trade of beatster. Much of her working life was spent mending herring lints either on various net-stores or on a part-time basis at home.

TED FROST (born 1901) – a shipwright by trade and a man of varied nautical experience. He spent several years at sea as a ship's carpenter. He has spent his retirement recording old shipbuilding practices for posterity.

CLIFFORD GOULDBY (1889–1977) – a member of a notable Kessingland fishing family, whose grandfather and father were both pillars of the industry. He went into business on his own account quite early on in life and was a leading herring merchant for many years.

HAROLD MITCHELL (1903–1985) – was engaged in the family fish-selling business for the whole of his working life and spent much of his working life following the fishing fleets round the coasts of Britain.

ARTHUR PITCHER (born 1905) – a long-serving employee of the East Anglian Ice Company who saw many developments over the course of his career in the use of ice and refrigeration in the fishing industry.

MINNIE PITCHER (born 1905) – spent her working life in a net making factory.

REGGIE REYNOLDS (born 1906) – a fish-curer whose family had long connections with the industry, both his father and uncle being well-known smokers.

BERT STUBBS (born 1903) – a member of a Gorleston fishing family, who served his time as a marine engineering apprentice with the Yarmouth firm of Crabtree. He was engineer of the volunteer lifeboat *Elizabeth Simpson* during the 1920s and later joined the Merchant Navy.

NEWHAM TIMM (1899–1984) – a life-long railwayman who began his transport career as a lad and worked his way up to station master. Much of his working life was spent in the Eastern Counties, the last stage in charge of Yarmouth Vauxhall.

STELLA WALPOLE (born 1900) – a member of a fishing family from the village of Corton. She spent a number of years during her teens and twenties working in the area's two main fish-canning factories.

ANNIE WATT (1892–1978) – a native of the coast of north-east Scotland, who spent the whole of her working life as a gutter and packer in the pickling yards. She and her husband travelled the British coasts in pursuit of the herring, before eventually settling in Suffolk. (Lowestoft Journal)

JAMES WATT (1892–1977) – awarded the M.B.E. for his services to the fishing industry. He was a foreman cooper for many years with various Scottish curing firms, his working life stretching from before the First World War to the herring's final decline in the 1960s. (Lowestoft Journal)

Scottish zulus and local sailing drifters leaving Yarmouth harbour about the turn of the century. All the boats are under tow from a tug – except the one on the far left, which has its mains'l hoisted and the crew busy on the sweeps.

CHAPTER ONE

Scotch Cure

'We've gutted fish in Lerwick and in Stornoway and Shields,
Worked along the Humber 'mongst the barrels and the creels.
Whitby, Grimsby, we've traivelled up an' doon,
But the place to see the herrin' is the quay at Yarmooth toon.'
(Scotch Girls' Song from 'Singing The Fishing' – Ewan MacColl and Charles Parker)

The so-called Scotch Cure of herrings was reputedly invented by a Dutchman towards the end of the 14th century. Wilhelm Beukels is given the credit for devising the technique of removing the gill and long gut and then packing the catches "sardine-fashion" in barrels, with a layer of salt between each tier of fish. There were many variations of this method down the years and it gave the Dutch an unrivalled and controlling share of the European herring trade throughout the 16th and 17th centuries. It wasn't until the 19th that the British fishing communities really began to make themselves felt on any significant scale. The decline of the Dutch had a lot to do with this and the reasons for their retraction from the North Sea in the post-Napoleonic period have often been debated.

Whatever the causes, there is no denying the vigour with which the British fishing industry expanded to fill the vacuum, aided also by the growing demand for fish in the industrial centres at home and by the development of the railways. Scotland's east coast particularly, burgeoned in the mid 19th century. By the 1860s the men from Fife were not only pursuing their summer voyage at home, but migrating southwards down the Yorkshire coast and eventually to East Anglia for the lucrative autumn fishing season. It was an exodus that grew every year, so that by the early 1900s (an era bolstered by the growth in numbers of steam drifters) a veritable invasion of Great Yarmouth and Lowestoft took place each September and October of fisher-folk from all round the Scottish coasts.

The most memorable feature of this invasion was the gangs of Scots fishing girls who followed the fleets of boats southwards to supply the seasonal shoreside labour needed to deal with the catches. Annie Watt (1892–1978) was a typical gutting-girl of her generation, who left her Peterhead home each year to go south, eventually marrying and settling in Lowestoft, as did many of them.

"In my mother's young time there was no Yarmouth fishin'. I first came tae Yarmooth when I was 15; I'm now 84. It was open denes, most of it, then. It was a cold fishin', but we never bothered about that. A lot o' the Scottish boats were sail boats and if you went oot o' Yarmouth with six, seven or eight pound wages, that was a big fishin' because a lot o' the time the boats couldna get oot o' harbour for the weather. The girls use tae walk from the denes back to their lodgins up Blackfriars Road, and there's one thing I can say, I'd always good lodgins in Yarmooth. Some o' them were terrible, but I always had good ones.

"Actually, the first year I came doon, I was in Gorleston. 1908 it was, and we came across from Ardglass, in Ireland, on the day o' the races. Yarmooth Races. It was a Saturday in September and we'd been over in Ireland, working there for seven weeks. We used tae go to Ireland in the winter time as well. I've seen me going oot o' Yarmooth, with just a few days at home for Christmas, and then I'd to go to Ardglass. We'd be 14 hours crossing over from Glasgow and you should have seen the boats! Not like the grand boats o' today. The boats we was going in then was cattle boats! I liked Ireland, though. The people were grand. We used tae go oot sledgin' with the boys in the snow, and we used tae go and walk in the hills as well. There was no covers over where we worked, not like Yarmooth and Lowestoft. We just used to work outside, gut and pack outside in the snow. But it was fun.

"When we came to Yarmooth and Lowestoft, we used tae come down by train. In the old days it only cost 30 shillings return. Ye never went to sleep. All the guttin' crews would be singing and dancing. We used tae have small spirit lamps and make tea in the train. Oh, it was fun. Ye never felt the time. I wish it was those days now. After that first year in Gorleston I came to Lowestoft until the year I married. 1913. Then I'd tae go to Yarmooth because o' my husband's work. Ye went where the work was. We were here in Lowestoft the first year after the 1914 War, working at the back o' Morton's Factory on the quay there, and we were here too the first year o' the last war. There was planes reconnoitring and the sailors was all here, and ye couldna hardly get lodgins.

"I was just past 13 when I went to start at the herrin'. Ye learnt yesel'. Ye'd just start the job and go along at it and then ye'd come into the speed. If you'd no speed, it was nae use – you couldna make much. When I was a girl in Peterhead, in the old days before the First War, a man would come round tae the house and tell ye that the herrin' would be in the yard at nine o'clock, and sometimes we didna stop till three or four o'clock the next morning. Gutting all the time. Ye got nothing tae eat unless someone brought it. We used tae send somebody across to the coffee shop for a flask o' tea and some pieces. And that was all ye got till ye went home next morning. Oh, I've seen me ganging home at three or four o' clock in the morning and mother would have bowls o' soup on for me, and the left-over dinner was always kept.

"In Yarmooth and Lowestoft we always worked down on the denes, and I've seen sail boats coming ashore with the storms. Washed ashore right up on the sands where we was working. We wore oilskin skirts and rubber boots. In my young day it was heavy leather boots, but then the rubber ones come in after the First War. The skirt fastened on the chest with straps and buttons and kept ye clean. You wore just cast-off clothes, old jackets and skirts and that. Good clothes was nae use because they'd get spoiled. Ye just washed out what ye wore and put them on again when they were dry. Some o' the landladies used to put brownpaper or oilcloth around the wall o' the lodgins, because some o' the girls were careless; they didna take off their dirty claes when they got in. Packing herrin' was the cleanest job. Ye'd only the salt tae worry about.

"With the gutting, ye didna cut yeself if ye tied your fingers right with bits o' rag. And the salt on the herrin' helped ye grip them. See, the coopers salted the fish as they were put into the farlane. But if your hands were cut – oh me, I've some of the marks yet going to my grave! It was the salt that did it. Oh aye, it would eat into your hands. In later years, when I was in Lerwick, I used rubber gloves. You needed a pair o' gloves every week, but that was nothing; it saved ye tying up your fingers all the time. We'd a big week there in Gorleston once when, between the Tuesday and the Friday, we did 288 barrels. I'd a good crew with me doing the gutting and I was packing. We used tae work till six o'clock one night and nine the next, but that week we worked till nine all four nights. There was such a big fishin' on the Tuesday that the boats couldna go back to sea all week. The curers were all filled up for the week and we just had tae gut the fish every day till they were all done. I tell ye, we made 288 barrels by the Friday night, gutting and packing every one."

Annie's reference to the boats not being able to fish for the rest of the week, after heavy landings on the Tuesday, places that bumper week in the mid 1930s. It was at this time, owing to the periodic gluts of herring and to the uncertainty of the market, that attempts were made to control the quantities of fish landed. Once the stipulated quota had been reached the drifters were not allowed out of harbour again until the catches had been cleared. With regard to Annie Watt's record week, it is interesting to note that at a good average rate of 50 to 60 herrings being gutted per minute by each of two girls, and with a barrel holding something like 1,000 fish, 96 solid working hours would have produced round about 280 to 290 barrels. Coincidence that the two figures should tally? Not really. Years of experience in any job usually result in an almost intuitive sense of what can be achieved in a given period of time.

"You worked in threes. Two gutted and one packed. Every girl that gutted had a gut tub – a little tub made with hoops the same way that barrels were – and the guts were put in there. It stood up beside the girl in the farlane and she flung her guts into it. When it was full, she just lifted it up and ran tae the gut barrel with it, because the guts were sold for fertiliser. In my early years it was all working deep *farlanes* and ye had to bend tae the bottom to get the herrin' out. But, then, in the latter years they raised the troughs to keep the women's backs straight. The farlane was up to the gutter's cut then and ye could get ahead faster.

"The herrin' were brought up by horse and cart or lorry, and sometimes they'd be in kits and sometimes they'd be loose. Once the herrin' were in the farlane, the coopers would salt them, and ye had tae salt them according to size. The bigger ones needed more salt than the smaller ones did. As ye gutted the herrin', you threw them into the different tubs which stood behind you. The different sizes went into different tubs and that was called selecting. You only had about three or four sizes down here in Yarmooth and Lowestoft because there wasn't a lot o' selections. Aye, ye could make more money gutting here than you could at hame on the Summer Fishing, because there was a lot more sizes in Scotland. That meant a lot more work and ye couldna go at the same speed as ye could down here.

"There used tae be about 900 to 1,200 herrin' in every barrel, according to size. The fish were always packed belly up and ye kept the heads tae the sides o' the barrel. Ye packed each tier at right-angles to the one below and ye sprinkled salt on every layer. There'd be about 20 tiers in a barrel when ye finished, but as the herrin' lie in the pickle they gradually go down. Ye see, the salt melts with the herrin' and that's what makes the pickle, but the fish shrink and go down. The coopers would open the barrel up and drain the pickle off through the bung-hole, then we'd tae fill it up with maybe three or four tiers o' herrin'. After we'd done that, the barrel would be headed up again, laid flat on the ground and the pickle poured back in. Ye did different cures as well. Some were heavy and some were fine. The *maatjes* were fine; they'd hardly any salt on them at all and the folk over there on the Continent were daft about them! Oh, there was a lot o' work in curing herrin'. In my young day among fisher-folk it was all the trade there was for girls. We liked it well enough, but it was hard work. I've seen me packing in a wilderness o' barrels – packing away from Monday morning till Saturday nicht. But ye had tae do it or ye'd make nothing."

During the years leading up to the First World War a barrel of good quality pickled herrings fetched up to about 35 shillings (£1·75). Tens of thousands of these barrels were exported each herring season from any one of the major fishing stations along the whole eastern coastline of Britain. They were shipped across to Germany, to Poland and to Russia, and on their successful sale depended the livelihood of numerous Scottish communities. The wages earned by the women may seem small today, but the money was vital in sustaining many families.

"All the years that ever we worked, till the end o' the First War, the price we got for a barrel o' herrin' was eightpence (3½p). Then it went up tae 1/2d (6p) for a time, before the fishing got kind o' dull and they took it down to tenpence (4p). The women went on strike in their droves because the pay had been cut. Oh, it was hard work. I told ye aboot the 288 barrels we had up tae Friday nicht from Tuesday – well, I had a flier of a crew there, gutters, and I was with them 15 years altogether. That time there in Gorleston, we only had the first day working fresh herrin'. The rest o' the week all the fish were roused, sprinkled with salt tae preserve them. Now, packing fresh herrins (especially them with the roes in) makes the barrels come up far faster than when you're packing salted ones. Oh aye, it does. Because once they're salted, it shrinks them.

"Each crew of three had their own money and shared it. Every crew's barrels were marked so ye could tell whose were whose. Yes, they were numbered. And when the herrin' had shrunk and ye had tae fill the barrels up, ye got threepence (1½p) an hour. Yes, you got paid eightpence a barrel and threepence an hour topping up, but you didna lift your earnings till the end o' the year. You had tae live on what the curers paid ye for lodgings and food. We got eight shillings (40p) a week before the First War and that was tae keep ye. The landladies didna make themselves rich off what they got, I'm telling ye! – we paid aboot three shillings (15p) or 3/6d (17½p) a week for lodgings and they cooked us food for that as well, though we'd tae buy it. The money we earnt might not seem a lot, but if ye went into service in them days you only got half-a-crown (12½p) a week, or perhaps three or four shillings (15 to 20p). So you were much better off going away on the fishing.

"It was hard, though. Aye, there was no *diet hours* before the First War. No, until after the war there was no *diet hours* – never in history! The men got no diet hours either; they used tae spell one another round and get a bite o' something that way. We used to order something at the coffee stall and have the woman bring it over, a cup o' watery tea and maybe a couple o' biscuits, and that was all ye had till ye went home. My mother used to have the bowls o' soup ready and we'd sit supping that till all hours o' the morning. After the war it changed. The first union started up our way and we got diet hours."

The concession gained regarding meal-times during the working day was an important one. Nevertheless, pickling herrings remained an arduous way of making a living and good lodgings were essential if the season was to pass reasonably well. As far as any real leisure time was concerned, only the weekend offered much chance for diversion and the girls were quick to take advantage of it. Many folk who either lived in fishing ports, or who visited them at such times as herring were being caught, will remember the way in which the many groups of Scottish lasses walked about town, their heads clad in shawls. Singing and laughter were the order of the day, but the noise was never made in mere idleness and all the while busy fingers knitted industriously.

"We never had much spare time, but when we did all the girls used tae go about knitting. Aye, they'd knit away. Sometimes we would be away of a Saturday nicht up tae the Yarmooth *Hipprodrome* or to one o' the other shows. Oh, there were grand shows in Yarmooth and we only used to pay about fourpence (2p) tae get in. We were never in much pocket money tae spend, but we could afford that. If we had a nicht off during the week, a bunch of us used tae walk from Gorleston to Yarmooth, but on a Saturday we'd catch the bus.

"Things were never as good with the herrin' after the First War. One curer we worked for went broke. That was David Buchan. He was one o' the richest curers in Peterhead and an honester man never walked! He'd a big house and everything, but he lost the lot. He'd plenty o' money owing tae him, but it was all in Germany and Russia. Nearly all the curers was in a bad way then. They were that bad that they couldna fix the women for the herrin'. See, they fixed the crews for the summer fishing during the winter. They paid ye about £3 fixing money (*arles*, we called it) and that bound ye to them; ye signed a paper to say so. Well, things were so bad at the time that the curers hadn't the money even to fix the crews. There was nae work for the coopers either. The herrin' trade was just at a standstill."

The cancellation by the Bolsheviks of foreign debts incurred by the Tsarist regime, plus the German monetary crisis of 1923, caused a great deal of hardship among Scottish curers. Mrs. Watt remembered the money owed and the loss of once-productive markets as clearly as everything else about her working life. James Watt (1892–1977), her husband, was a foreman-cooper of great skill and long experience whose services to the fishing industry were acknowledged in 1973 when he was awarded the British Empire Medal.

"You started your apprenticeship at the coopering and ye served four years. Your money was four shillings (20p) a week the first year, then five (25p), six (30p), and eight shillings (40p) the last year. It was hard work, I'm telling ye. All muscle and no brain. Brute strength and stupidity. But there was nae much else in Peterhead at the time. When I first begun, my employer gave me a cooper's tool set. 'Free o' charge,' he said. But he got his money back all right. I had tae make an extra barrel a week over the whole o' the four years to pay for it. Well, by the time I'd finished my apprenticeship, he'd had something like 200 tae 250 extra barrels oot o' me, hadn't he? Well, that paid for the tool kit he gave me. The whole thing was just hard work and speed. I remember me going doon Broad Street in Peterhead the week before I got married, 1913 – it was three o' clock in the morning and I'd made 72 barrels that week for two pound, seven and something (£2.35 or so). 72 barrels! Once I was a journeyman, though, I didna stay coopering for too long. I did not! I became a foreman in the pickling yard, because it was a better job.

"We used tae come doon tae Lowestoft and Yarmooth on the train. Sometimes we came on buses, but that was after the First War. We used tae get here about the time o'

Yarmooth Races and we'd go back home about the beginning o' December. Local men made a lot o' the barrels doon here at Yarmooth and Lowestoft. It wasna all done by us. There was a barrel factory in Yarmooth, just afore ye go over the bridge and one man I knew used tae walk there to work from Gorleston every day. A lot o' Scotch fellers settled down here too – married English girls and got a job making barrels.

"I was earning £1. 18s. (£1.90) a week in 1912 and you'd to pay your own board and lodgings oot o' that, perhaps eight or nine shillings (40 to 45p) a week. I was single then, so the food was thrown in. I was working for the firm o' W. Slater & Sons, one o' the biggest curing firms in the trade, and that was the year we hoisted the flag. We cured 100,000 barrels o' herrin' and we hoisted a flag in our yard. Oh aye, and we all got a gold half-sovereign. My father was buying herrin' for the same firm that year and his first day's buying in the season went tae 960 cran. We had 20 crews o' girls in one yard and 20 in the other, and by God we had tae work! We'd be starting at six o' clock in the morning and going right through.

"The timber for the barrel staves was spruce and they came all ready tae use. Same with the ends; they came ready-made as well: three pieces o' spruce dowelled together and rounded off, with the bottom end thicker than the top one. We got all our stuff from Aberdeen. I never made barrels here in Lowestoft, but it would have been the same thing – Swedish spruce or something like that coming in on a cargo boat. The staves were 31½ inches long and four inches wide, though I've known the width to vary from as much as five inches to about three and a half. We'd half-barrels too, as well as the big ones. And firkins. The end hoops were always steel (except in my father's day, when they were wood), but the quarter-hoops varied. There the wooden ones made o' ash and they had to be steeped in water for a week before bending. Oh aye, they had. Then you'd take the adze and cut a lip at each end, so they fitted over, and pin them with three nails. Now, the other type o' quarter-hoop was made o' steel and had a raised middle."

There was parliamentary legislation going back to the reign of George the Third to stipulate the size of barrels used in the trade for pickled herrings. The barrel was reckoned at 26⅔ Imperial gallons, the half-barrel at 13⅓ and the quater-barrel (or firkin) at 6⅔ Very strict regulations were laid down as well regarding the pickling process itself and two of the foreman cooper's chief responsibilities were to see that the quality of the fish was of the highest standard and that the sizing of individual categories (there were seven of these in all) was accurate. The Scottish Fishery Board required its officers to inspect at least four out of every hundred barrels made.

"Once the barrels were made the foreman would inspect them tae see that they were air-tight. If ye did find a barrel leaking pickle, you'd remove the end hoop, force the staves apart with a *flagging-iron* and put a length o' steeped rush in the join. Then ye'd bring the staves together again and put the end hoop back on. That would be enough tae seal it usually. See, the herrin' made their own pickle in the barrel and ye wanted tae keep everything just right. There was different types o' pickled herrins and different sizes as well. The *maatje* herrin' were very popular over in Germany. That was a very light cure with just a fine sprinkling o' salt. Other pickles would be going out tae Finland, Russia and other places. They were shipped out on cargo boats and before the First War I suppose they'd fetch about 35 shillings (£1.75) a barrel.

"When the girls started work at the gutting, they'd got tae learn up. You'd put three girls together, just learning, and the men would guide them. They'd all be the same age, ye see, just learning, and the coopers would watch them until they'd got broken in tae the selections. You had tae watch all the girls at the farlanes, especially on the summer fishing at home. See, there'd be perhaps seven or eight tubs for each crew (square box things they put the herrin' in) and that meant a different size o' fish for each tub. They were all different selections – matties, matfulls, fulls, large fulls – and you might get some girls throwing them in the wrong tubs.

"My wife always says I was the worst foreman she had! But I couldna be showing any favourtism now, could I? One o' the biggest things aboot being foreman was the girls! They'd fall out many, many times. Then if you were maybe getting on to them aboot not doing their work right, they'd start to throw the tears. Oh, murder! But it was fair enough – bad gutters and bad packers could ruin a firm. Oh, gosh aye! Too much salt in the herrins; not packing them right; bulking. I'll tell ye what bulking is. It's when a girl packed a barrel the right way up tae a certain level, then threw a whole lot o' herrin' in just anyhow. It made the barrel come up quicker, ye see. Then she'd pack the last few tiers properly to finish with. Oh, there was quite a few of them got copped doing that."

The foreman cooper had to be vigilant because his firm's success depended on the quality of its product. North of the Border this was, in turn, was guaranteed by the Scottish Fishery Board after rigorous checks by qualified inspectors. Once the standard of the pickled herrings was deemed acceptable, the barrels were branded with an outline of a crown, containing the word 'Scotland', and showing the size of fish, the initials of the curer and the year. It was a system operated only in Scotland and it specified seven individual categories of herring: *Large Full* (big fish, full of milt and roe and not less than 11¼ inches long); *Full* (fish with milt and roe in them, not less than 10¼ inches long); *Large Spent* (fish that had spawned, not less than 10 inches long); *Filling* (maturing fish, not less than 10¼ inches long); *Medium* (maturing fish, not less than 9½ inches long); *Matfull* (fish with milt and roe in them, not less than 9¼ inches long); *Mattie* (young maturing fish, not less than 9 inches long).

"With the Fishery Brand o' herrin' we had inspectors coming round the yards looking at the fish, and if we'd got any faults they'd chuck 'em. You know, refuse to pass them. Now, if they did that, your boss would maybe lose seven to ten shillings (35 to 50p) on every barrel. When an inspector came into the yard, ye gave him a piece o' chalk and he'd mark oot which barrels he wanted to check. They'd all be standing in tiers and you'd pull oot the ones he marked. Some would be head up, others bottom up, so you'd take the heads or bottoms oot for him and put that tier o' herrin' in a little tub for him tae go through. He'd look to see if there was any herrin' too small or too thin, or anything like that. There might be too much salt on 'em. He could reject 'em for that. Now, the bottom tier was always the best tier in the barrel (the foreman always inspected that one himself to make sure it was first-class) but the inspector would pick through it just the same. There was one feller there at Peterhead who was called 'Bunghole Willie', or something like that, because he'd go that far doon in a barrel just to see if he could catch the girls bulking.

"Once ye'd got a good inspection, the Fishery Officer would say, 'Righto, brand away.' So you'd pack the herrins he'd taken oot back into the barrels and head the barrels up again. Then you'd brand all the barrels you'd got stacked and waiting. You had an iron thing with a crown on it, and the dates and everything, and it was heated in a fire. You put this on the bilge of the barrel, so the brand could be seen, whoever comes. The firm's name was stencilled on the head. They went mostly to Germany, the Crown Brand herrin', but there was none of it done in England. No, you'd no Fishery Officers doon here. What ye had was the firms' inspectors – you know, people working for the firms buying the herrin'. They weren't quite as particular as the Fishery Officers, but they were canny fellers."

Apart from the actual Crown Brand varieties of herring, there was another standard of excellence which enjoyed a high reputation in the industry. This was known as *Trademarking* and it was an accolade given to curers who were of such an impeccable reputation that their product was its own guarantee of excellence. The *Trademarkers*, as they were known, were set apart from the *Ordinaries* by being allowed to let their own individual stencil-marks act as the confirmation of quality. Such recognition did not come easily. It had to be worked for and, once achieved, needed to be most carefully maintained.

"I was foreman seven years with John Sutherland. Now, he was a first-class trademarker. So was Andrew Duncan, and I was seven years along o' him. W. Slater & Sons was another good trademark; my father was manager o' that firm for years. You used tae stencil the trademark on the barrels, but they'd still be inspected before they went oot o' the yard. Oh aye. You'd have the customer's inspector pick out the ones he wanted and go through 'em. I was foreman for three years for a feller called Robertson Buchan. He had five crews work for him, 15 girls, and he was a great lad for buying good herrin'. We had three shots o' herrin' come inta the market there one day at Peterhead and he bought one of 'em. They were lovely herrin', all large fulls and fulls, and there wasna one o' the gutters left the farlane all day. They were gutting all the time and the packer was even emptying their guts into the gut barrel. The large fulls that we cured all went to America; that was the best market for big herrin'.

"The whole secret o' the business was in the pickling. After the barrels had been packed, they'd be tiered up and left tae stand. And from the day the herrin' were gutted till the day the barrels were filled up ready to send off was ten days. Aye, they'd to be standing ten days to let the pickle make. The process was called pining and the Fishery Board regulations was ten days from the day ye gutted the herrin' till the day ye filled the barrels up. After the girls had packed the barrels, the coopers would come along and put them away. The barrels were stood on top of each other, three tiers high. After the ten days were up, they'd be taken doon and the bung-hole put in. Ye used an *auger* to bore through with, about three inches above the bottom quarter-hoop. The hole was about an inch to an inch and a quarter in diameter, tapering inwards. After that was done, two of the men stood the barrel up again; the head was taken out; and the pickle poured oot into a tub. Ye kept that to use again because ye could never make fresh pickle as good as the original stuff. Then the girls would come along tae do the filling.

"The barrels were filled with herrin' o' the same size and length o' cure as the ones already in, then ye'd head them up again. Once that was done, the fillers would pour the pickle back in through the bung-hole. Then ye'd stop the hole with a wooden plug, a bung, which would be a good tight fit. No leak. When I was in Ullapool once, some o' the old fishermen that was there had been curing a few herrin' for the winter. And they were telling me what they did. 'Oh,' says one, 'we always throw oot the old pickle and put in fresh.' So I says to them, 'I've been in this trade long enough tae give ye some advice. Ye're just making a mess of it, because the pickle ye're throwing oot is the original stuff. You're taking oot the best pickle and putting in the worst.' So after that they stopped doing it their way and did it right. I was 12 years in Ullapool, buying herrin', and I liked it. Aye, I was well content there.

"I was in charge o' Donald Macrae's yard for 15 years and we did kippers as well as the pickled herrin'. We were doon on the Whapload Road in Lowestoft and we'd three machines there for splitting herrin'. This was between the wars and they'd do 54 herrins a minute, them machines. We just used to take the herrins oot, wash 'em, pickle 'em and then hang 'em up in the *kells*. We dyed the fish, but not too heavy. A kipper is better tae eat with a touch o' dye on it than one with no dye at all, and the reason is this: it takes the smoke better than an undyed one and doesna have tae be in the kell so long, a-drying up. We smoked our kippers over oak shavings and sawdust and we did 80 to 100 crans o' herrin' a day. Oh aye. We used tae sell the milts by the stone dearer than we did the kippers! We did bucklings as well. They were herrin' with the heads taken off and hung up by the tail in a kind of oven. There was hardly any smoke at all, just heat, so they were like a cooked herrin'. They were very popular with the drivers. 'Jimmy,' one would say. 'I've eaten ten *bucklings*.' Ten! That'd be for dinner.

"We used tae do Norwegian herrin' as well. We used to kipper them in Fraserburgh and at Fairlie, doon on the Clyde. They were big herrin' and you'd a terrible job tae get them into the one-stone boxes ye used. Ye couldna put them across, they were that long. They all went abroad, them big herrin'. They were shipped over in big wooden cases, in ice, and they were murder tae lift. It would be the winter time and your hands were cold, cold. I've seen Donald Macrae's lorries down at North Shields for the herrin' coming in from Norway and they used tae take them back up tae Fraserburgh to kipper. I was with that firm a long time. They've a big place now, aboot a mile out o' Fraserburgh.

"It seems a long while now since I first came tae Lowestoft. It was in 1919 and we were working in Belvedere Road, at the back o' the Belvedere pub – right on the quay there. It used tae be very busy in Lowestoft once you were a-going right; the Hamilton Dock used tae be full up with Scottish boats. This year we were working in Belvedere Road, the boats used tae come right up beside ye and put the herrin' right into the farlanes. Oh aye, there was no carting. I was working for David Buchan, the most honest curer there was. He died penniless in the end – got a big smack in Russia and Germany. No money. I'll tell ye how honest he was. We let a shot of *overdays* go over tae Germany as fresh herrin' that year in Belvedere Road and he was very angry aboot it. There was nothing wrong with 'em (they were lovely fish and they passed the inspection), but they were overdays and he was going tae let them go at a lesser price. He wasna pleased that we'd let 'em go as fresh. In the end he lost all his money in Russia and Germany, with the Revolution and with the mark being nae use."

James Watt's reference here is to 1923 when inflation went through the roof in Germany and many British exporters suffered. The Scottish curers have all gone now, as have most of the coopers and gutting girls.

Scottish fisher girls gutting herrings in Yarmouth before 1914. Working long hours in all weathers, many of them could gut at the rate of one fish per second.

CHAPTER TWO

The Klondyke Trade

'Wha'll buy my caller herrin'?
They're bonnie fish an' halesome farin';
Wha'll buy my caller herrin'
New drawn frae the Forth?'
('Caller Herrin'' – Baroness Nairne)

As the name *Klondyke* suggests, this particular aspect of the herring trade was roughly contemporaneous with the Yukon gold-rush of the 1890s and led to a considerable amount of money being earned by those people involved in it. It was actually started by a man called Benjamin S. Bradbeer who, while visiting friends in Hamburg during the year 1887, noticed just how great the German demand for fresh herrings was. Imports of Norwegian fish were prominent on the wharves of Hamburg and enquiries among the merchants there as to the possibility of shipping out Lowestoft herrings met with a courteous response.

On his return to Lowestoft, Mr. Bradbeer duly shipped out some small quantities of autumn herring and these met with such an enthusiastic reaction that the demand in Germany very quickly built up to a considerable level. Altona became the port of reception and, in due course, representatives of the various German importers began to come over to England. Until the First World War the fish were shipped across on specially chartered steamers in wooden kits (iced and lightly salted), but when trade resumed again after the conflict timber cases were used. These made the handling of the herrings much easier, and the large dumps of them which stood around town awaiting use were a notable feature of the Lowestoft scene during the 1920s and 30s. Ernie Armes (born 1902) worked for one of the German klondyke firms throughout this period.

"Klondykin' was started by a Low'stoft merchant, old Ben Bradbeer. He was across in Hamburg and that went through his brainbox, 'Well, they could probably do with some herrins here.' His firm were shipbrokers and one thing and another, and fish merchants, so he made application to one or two blokes he knew in Hamburg to see if he could send some herrins over. That was old Boettcher an' Schumacher an' them, the same names as when I was klondykin'. Then, when he got back to Low'stoft, he went in with Mr. Edward Gouldby and his son, Mr. Arthur Gouldby (that'd be Cliffie Gouldby's grandfather and father), and the trade gradually built up.

'When I first started on the Low'stoft market, in 1919, I worked for Mr. Arthur Evans, one o' the biggest trawl-fish merchants down there, an' I was with him till about 1925. Things got very shaky then in the fish-trade and he went bang. A lot o' good firms did. Anyway, I was out of a job and I'd just got married, so I had to git somethin' quick. I was lucky; I managed to jump inta the klondykin'. I knew an old boy who was in it an' he give me the tip-orf. The German firms used to come over for the Home Fishin', yuh see, and there was quite a few of 'em: Figena, Hilligaart, Selimer, Franze Witte, Arthur Schillen,

Arthur Koser, and the rest.

"I got a job with Figena. They had a big factory in Altona and all the fish they bought was took over there. The bulk o' the kondyke firms were sendin' their herrins on to the Altona commission market, or on to the Hamburg one, and they'd be sold there as fresh herrins. The November herrin' was what they liked to buy; they used to step in heavy on them. They'd built up bloomin' good European markets, had the Germans, and they used to send herrins all over the show – Czechoslovakia, Bulgaria, and places like that. A lot o' the herrins what were shipped over to Cuxhaven and Bremerhaven went to Czechoslovakia and we used to put a special mark on the boxes. That was a damn good trade, until Hitler started playin' the bloomin' fool and brought the war on.

"The Poles and the Russians never had nothin' to do with klondykin'. No, it was all Scotch cure stuff with them. The barrels used to go to Stettin and all them places up there. Danzig. There was no klondykin' to Holland or Belgium either. They used to cure their own. Some o' the firms here used to send *rough packs* over to Ostend. Oh yeah, there was a trade for them. See, they weren't pickled properly; they were just shoved into kits with plenty o' salt on and then shipped across. The firm of N. H. Catchpole used to do a lot of them. You'd git one or two Dutch firms comin' over here as well. Old Jacobson was one. He used to bring his own Dutch coopers with him and they used to do rough pack herrins.

"Like I said, the firm I worked for, Figena, had their own factory and they used to make various things out o' the herrin'. Some would go to make fish paste, some would be turned inta bucklins, and some would be tinned. Then they used to put some in little glass jars, all split and rolled up nice with bay leaves. Very often they used to send a sample across for us chaps to eat, and they were very, very good. Everything connected with the herrin' what this factory handled had a use. The scales were cleaned and made inta various things, like artificial pearls and dolls' eyes and all little things like that. All the bones were crushed up and went to make fertiliser or glue, so there was nothin' wasted at all. They did *roll-mops* out there as well, but a different way to how they were done in England. There used to be one firm in Low'stoft do a lot o' roll-mops. That was F. H. Phillips from North Shields and they used to send a lot o' their stuff over to America. The herrins were done in a kind of sweet vinegar, with bay leaves, and we used to call it the *Jew-Boy Trade*.

"The German buyer wanted a good class o' herrin' for the klondyke. Once he'd bought a catch and that was bein' unloaded from the drifter, his eye would be a-lookin' all round. He'd keep pickin' the fish up, and if they weren't good enough he'd chuck 'em up. Scaled herrins were no good at all. No. You used to git a lot o' them when they'd bin trawled up and they were mostly put inta tins. The Klondyke trade was mostly honest. Definitely. I mean, the bulk o' the blokes knew they were on a good job, so they looked out to keep it. And the firms had their reputations to think of as well. The herrins used to be landed in quarter-cran baskets and the fisherman would sometimes try to play a game with yuh. They might have some overdays on board, say, and they'd try to land them in among the fresh. You soon got to know about all them sorts o' tricks, though. If any overdays did slip through, because you weren't careful enough, they soon found out across on the other side. Yeah, they knew over there in Altona all right, and they'd be on the phone straight away and blow the buyer up about it. If any o' the blokes got caught on the Low'stoft market letting overdays slip through, they'd git the sack straight away.

"The klondyke boxes what we used to put the herrin' in were what we called seven in four. That was seven baskets o' herrin' inta four boxes. The baskets held a quarter-cran each, so that meant the boxes held under half a cran. The herrins were sold by weight when they got over to the Altona commission market and each box was supposed to hold about 180 pounds o' herrin'. See, a quarter-cran o' herrin' weighed seven stone, so the seven inta four worked out about the right amount. The way we used to work was to put down 16 boxes on the ground and put seven cran o' herrin' in 'em. Then we'd put another 16 boxes on top o' them – another seven cran. Then, on top o' that lot, would go another 16 – another seven cran. So you finished up with 21 cran o' herrin' and three boxes high, which was as much as the fishermen could lift the baskets up to as we stood there saltin' the fish. That all depended on the class o' herrin' as to how much salt you put on. If they were a soft herrin', like from the Shetlands, you'd have to give 'em a little bit more salt. But a nice hard herrin', like you got on the east coast here, you'd give about a plateful to a basket. They had to be just finely sprinkled, and you had what was called a salt-plate and a kit o' salt to work from. Two fishermen used to lift up the basket o' fish and they'd stand one each side o' the box and shoot 'em out as you salted. There'd be ice in the box as well, o' course.

"We handled sprats and mackerel sometimes. When there was heavy landings o' sprats in Low'stoft, we'd send praps 30 boxes o' sprats on top of a cargo of herrin'. You used to sprinkle just a little salt over 'em (what was called pigeon-feed 'em) and then put ice on top. We'd take mackerel as well, if they were good. Yeah. Some o' the drifters would have, say, four or five baskets o' mackerel in among the herrin' and we'd buy 'em. There used to be a layer of fine ice put on the bottom o' the box and then the mackerel would be laid on that, belly up. You dint use no salt on mackerel and there'd be a layer of ice between each layer o' fish till you'd filled the box up.

"That used to be all go on the Low'stoft market durin' the Hoom Fishin'. You'd be saltin' and icin' the fish away; and as soon as you'd put the layer of ice on top to finish with, away come the nailing-down gang to put the lid on. Bang, bang, bang, and straight onto the sack-barrer. Then you'd have a gang o' blokes runnin' the boxes out to the cart. That was all done on the Herrin' Market. You done 'em in the front where the fish was landed and you run 'em straight out the back to where the cart was waitin'. Sometimes that was so crowded down there that I've klondyked on the road at the back o' the market.

"A lot o' blokes in Low'stoft used to git casual work on the klondykin'. Yeah, they'd come down the market and push a barrer about. Some o' the men employed in the railway's harbour yard used to come down about four or five o' clock in the mornin' and git a casual job for about three or four hours afore they started work. You put one box on a barrer and you'd be goin' backwards and forwards, backwards and forwards, a-loadin' 'em up. A horse and cart used to take about 16 boxes, but a lorry would carry double that – 30 or 32, praps.

"When the fishin' was in full swing, I've seen nothin' but carts and lorries right from the market, all the way along Battery Green Road, right the way round Waveney Road, leave a space in the High Street for the traffic, start again at Commercial road, go right the way down and come back up again to the bridge. Night after night after night that used to be like that. And as one cart unloaded onto the steamer, another one would pull up. The poor old horses used to be standin' for so long that they'd go to sleep and fall down with a wallop. There used to be two places to load the steamships up – just to the east o' the bridge and at a wharf up-through-bridge, near the dry-dock. Do yuh know, we used to load two ships in a day and a night! And they'd each hold about 6,500 boxes. There was always one boat kept in reserve, too, so that when the other two were away you'd could start loadin' up the third one.

"That was mainly horses and carts when I first started klondykin'. Then, as time went on, more and more lorries come in. I remember one year when some o' the carters went on strike. Yeah, that'd be about 1935. They went on strike for a little bit o' overtime pay and everything come to a standstill. See, a carter got praps 30 or 35 bob (£1.50–£1.75) a week and a lorry-driver praps ten bob (50p) more. Anyway, they come out on strike and the employers had to do somethin'. In the end they offered the blokes ninepence (4p) an hour after seven o' clock at night. Not extra! Cor blimey, no! Just ninepence an hour. And that's what they went on strike for.

"Just after the First World War there was a scheme to put food inta Germany under a kind o' Save The Children thing. They used to load up English trawlers with herrins here in the yacht basin and run 'em across to Altona. Then, when things got goin' again, a group of English merchants – Walter Wood-Greaves, Charlie Warner, Sayer & Holloway, Tom Brown, Edgar Clack and one or two more – formed the British Fresh Herring Exporters Association to start orf the klondykin' once more. And when the trade had been goin' for a year or two, the German firms started to come back over. They weren't allowed to buy their own herrin' at first, though; they had to employ an English agent. For instance, Walter Wood-Greaves was agent for Hilligaart, Billy Harvey acted for Arthur Koser, and so on. Then, after a year or two, that faded away and the Germans bought their own.

"During the 1920s, when the mark was bad, the people over here let the Germans always be a cargo of herrin' behind. In other words, they would buy the herrins and ship 'em over, but before the money for that cargo was paid they were allowed to start buyin' again. They were always that one cargo in debt, but the trade was kept goin'. Then, after a while, things levelled orf and became all right again. For a time, anyway, because there was a period in the early 1930s when the whole o' the fish trade was very, very sticky. Not just the herrins – everything. I mean, look at the fish merchants in Low'stoft what went through, some of 'em the big, old-established firms like Arthur Gouldby and Tom Brown. Sayer & Holloway, they went through, and they used to employ about 100 kipper girls! After the Second World War things got better, but the klondykin' never got goin' again. I think Bloomfield's o' Yarmouth (they were part o' the Unilever Group) tried it for about two years, then it collapsed."

In spite of the economic troubles of the 1920s and 30s, and with many other branches of the fishing industry in considerable difficulties, the Klondyke trade managed to stay reasonably stable. There was, it seemed, in Germany at least, a consistent market for supplies of fresh herrings which could be processed in a variety of ways, according to demand. Both at ordinary consumer level and in the gourmet sector of the food industry, herring products maintained their popularity. It was fortunate that high quality fish were required, because the German fishing fleet itself was mainly geared to trawling for herring – a method that led to catches being damaged. Drift-netting was far less destructive and thus Britain remained the primary source for top-quality herrings. Even during two decades of financial uncertainty, it is perhaps significant that German herring-traders paid their British workforce rather better than British fish-merchants remunerated their own employees.

"A lot o' the English merchants never really bothered about their men. The last thing they parted with was a decent wage. The German firms paid the best wages. Their ordinary rate was better and they paid 1/9d (9p) an hour overtime instead o' 1/6d (7½p). Also, with the Germans your overtime began at five p.m., where with the English people it was six. I knew one certain well-known herrin' buyer here in Low'stoft who had his son put the clock back when that'd nearly got to six o' clock. The blokes had about another quarter of an hour's work left to do, so he had the boy put the clock back by that quarter! When one o' the chaps got up to the Fox And Hounds, where he always went for a pint after work, he wondered why the pub clock was so fast. He soon found out! But what could you say? If you opened your mouth, you got the sack. There was no unions in them days down on the market, so you had to bite your tongue.

"With the German firms you got a pretty good wage, but you had to work hard for it. Blimey, there was times durin' the Hoom Fishin' when I left the house on a Wednesday night and dint see my missus again till late on the Saturday. The oldest boy and the second boy, they used to come down the market and bring me a bottle o' tea. When I did git hoom, I'd been down there so long that the wife had to wash me. I just fell asleep, so she washed me where I sat. Mind yuh, the one good thing about workin' at Low'stoft was that it was one o' the easiest klondyke ports to manage. Nearly every other port you went to, you had to lift the boxes up onta the cart or the lorry. But in Low'stoft you just used to run 'em out o' the back o' the market on the barrer an' put 'em straight on. See, the market is raised up, so that made for easier workin'.

"We never went to Yarmouth very much because that was very nearly all Scotch Cure over there. We used to go over an' buy a few herrins if there was a short supply in Low'stoft. That was bloomin' hard work over there, too! All the herrin' were sold in the old swill baskets over there an' you had to shoot 'em out inta boxes an' then lift the boxes up onta the lorry. There were about six quarter-cran baskets to a couple o' swills from what I can remember. The Scotchmen were the ones who made Yarmouth the port it was, yuh know. Cor, there used to be some big curin' yards over there.

"Our foreman at Low'stoft was an old boy called Harry Winters. He was a Grimsby man an' he'd been in the klondyke trade for years and years. He could hardly read or write, but he could tell yuh what part o' the North Sea nearly every bloomin' herrin' came from, just by lookin' at it. Cor he was a rum un. He sacked a bloke one day for stoppin' to roll a fag as he was pushin' a barrer. 'You can't do two jobs at once,' he said, so he paid him for the time he'd done an' give him the sack. Then, another time, he sacked one o' the blokes for goin' to git somethin' to eat about eight o' clock one Saturday night. This chap hadn't had anything all day, so I told him to go and git himself somethin'. He come back eatin' a cheese roll and ol' Harry Winters saw him. 'Eat! Eat, you booogger!' he say. 'You've got all Sunday to eat. Git orf home.' That was the same bloke who asked him for some oil one day to oil the wheels on his barrer with. 'Oil your barrer, you booogger,' he say. 'You want to oil your heels, you'd go a lot quicker then!' The ol' boy retired the year the Second World

War broke out, and I was goin' to take over from him. Yeah, I got his job and bloody war broke out! Marvellous!

"With the klondykin' you managed to keep workin' most o' the year round, though sometimes you got stood orf between the different seasons. When that happened, you got paid about thirty bob (£1.50) a week retainer till things got started again. After you'd finished the Shetland fishin', you came back to Low'stoft to start box-makin' ready for the Autumn Voyage here. You'd want somethin' like 30,000 to 40,000 boxes for that and the wood used to come over in sets from Norway and Germany. We used to get ours from Wenn o' Yarmouth, the timber merchants, and make 'em up on Battery Green, where the car park now is. 85 a day is what we made, for 55 bob (£2.75) a week. Now, that may not sound a lot, but there was about 70 nails in each box and you'd gotta make 'em properly. Ol' Harry Winters would inspect 'em. If there was one he didn't like the look of, he'd pull it down out o' the stack and kick the side out. 'What's up wi' this boogger?' he'd say and then you'd gotta re-nail it."

Up till now the klondyker's story has been almost wholly concerned with Lowestoft and the East Anglian autumn season, but some regular klondyke hands were every bit as migrant in their work routine as the fishermen themselves. In fact, they spent more of the year away in Scotland and Shetland than they did at home in Lowestoft, beginning the year on the coast of Ayrshire, moving across to the Firth of Forth in the spring and finishing at Lerwick during the summer.

"We generally used to leave Low'stoft either about the last week in December or the first week in January and go to the west side o' Scotland. We used to catch the rattler here and go up to Glasgow, and then from there you'd go across to Gourock or Ayr, or praps drop down to Girvan and Maidens and them little places. You used to find your own digs and I dint mind bein' up there at all – except it was winter time and blinkin' cold! The pub we used to use in Gourock, Cleat's Bar, did salt herrins out o' the vat for people to eat. Yeah, you could git these boiled salt herrins at a penny each, a penny hunk o' bread and a big boiled potato. The ol' girl in the pub had one o' them Valor Perfection oil stoves and she used to cook everything up on that. I've had many a dinner in there – boiled herrins, boiled spuds and a pint o' beer. That used to be lovely. O' course, the more herrins you ate, the more you wanted to drink! But we dint mind that.

"We used to set on local blokes wherever we went for humpin' the boxes and loadin' the lorries. You'd pay a man to do seven or eight hours work, say, and praps give him a quid. In Ayr the labour exchange wasn't far from where we worked and a lot o' the blokes we'd set on used to leave the job for just a little while to go and sign on the dole. 'Hi, Jimmy,' they'd say, 'I shan't be long. I'm just goin' to sign on.' We never took no names, yuh see. We just paid 'em the money. They were nice herrins round on that west side and they were mostly caught by ring-netters. There weren't many o' the Low'stoft boats got round there, though Jack Breach tried a little voyage durin' the 1930s. The *Girl Gladys* (LT 1174) went, so did the *Eileen Emma* (LT 342) and the *Swiftwing* (LT 675) and one or two more. They used one o' the boats to ship the herrins into and run 'em across to Ayr.

"You used to git a lovely little firm plump herrin' at the mouth o' the Clyde. Then the further you went up The Minch, up towards Stornoway, the herrins got bigger. We used to run up all the west side lochs, yuh know – Loch Fyne, Loch Linnhe, Loch Leven, Loch

Boisdale, right up to Kinlochbervie. We used to buy herrins orf the little crofters and load 'em loose straight inta big German trawlers that'd be waitin' up there. Then, after about four or five years, we started to klondyke 'em properly inta boxes and take 'em back down to Ayr or Gourock. They used to go overland then to Grangemouth, by rail, and be loaded aboard the German freighters, the *Hilde Bismarck* and all them.

"When we went on that fishin', we either used to take a motor lorry and travel round from loch to loch, or hire a little ol' puffer out from Gourock. That was a little ol' steamboat what used to go round all the little lochs and islands. We used to buy herrins orf the crofters, ice 'em down well on board, and then box 'em up properly when we got back to Gourock. The boat we usually went on was called the *Sunnyside*, and quite often you'd be on her in one o' the lochs after dark and you'd see a light a-comin' at yuh. Well, that'd be one o' the crofters in his boat and he'd got praps 20 or 30 baskets o' herrin' on board. He'd bin ring-nettin' for 'em, yuh see, him and his missus and praps a boy. Or praps he might just have had a couple or three drift nets out. Anyway, they'd come up past yuh in their boat and you'd shout out your price. You wanted to git herrins anywhere, so you dint mind buyin' little quantities like that. Blast, I've even bin up as far as Stornoway after 'em!

"That was a hard life, travellin' the coast, what with havin' to keep two hooms goin'. And that was better for a young feller than an older man. Yes, if you were single, that wasn't so bad – but if you were married, you never had much money. If that hadn't been for the overtime we used to git and the little bit o' *scran,* we sometimes wouldn't have had enough for a packet o' fags. Our money was £3.10s. (£3.50) a week and I used to send the missus £2. That used to go through the post, registered, for about 10d (4½ p). Then I had to pay about 25 bob (£1.25) a week for digs, so that'll tell yuh what I had left. This would be about 1930 time, right up till the war broke out. Some o' the digs were a bit rough and they'd probably only be about £1, but 25 bob was about the usual. You got everything for that – breakfast, dinner and tea – and if you couldn't git hoom for your dinner, then you got a damn good supper later on.

"After the west side fishin' was over, we used to go across to the Firth o' Forth – Anstruther, Pittenweem, St. Monance and them places. Yeah, we'd move over there about the beginnin' or the middle o' April. Anstruther was one o' my favourite ports. I actually used to lodge at Pittenweem, the middle one o' the three. I was with a woman there who was a rare good ol' sort. She was a good woman she was – as clean as wax and good food. When you were on the mainland, on that east side, there would always be a little buyer or two who you could make the odd shillin' from on the side. You know, they'd buy odd amounts o' leftover herrin' from yuh. We called 'em scran buyers. The most celebrated one in Anstruther was a little ol' fat lady called Mother Mimms. She was a nice ol' girl and she worked in with her daughter. She used to go round with a creel on her back and she'd give yuh about sixpence (2½ p) for a dozen herrins. Well, that was all right because you done that three or four times a day, and that was your beer money.

"I remember one year, when I was at Anstruther, we got news that there was some herrins bein' landed by miners at a place called Broughty Ferry. Thass near Dundee and the coal-miners had little boats there. Our German buyer, Martin Puzzel, made arrangements for us to go over on a lorry and git what we could. When we got there, the first place we went to was the pub – to git all the news. Then we went down to a sort o' grit beach where there was all these herrins. A lot of 'em were what we called seeds, very small, and we dint want them. But the biguns were all right. So what we done was to offer these miners four bob (20p) a quarter-cran basket for the biguns, only they had to sort 'em out. They dint mind doin' that because they'd bin ring-nettin' for these herrin' and that was beer money for 'em. When they'd done, we loaded the lorry up and went back to Anstruther.

"This ol' Martin Puzzel I just mentioned, he'd worked for Figena for a long time. In fact, he'd bin comin' over to this country for various klondyke firms ever since about 1898. He got interned here durin' the First World War. He wuz in Grimsby buyin' herrins in 1914 and he dint go hoom when he had the chance. He never thought such a thing could happen – England and Germany goin' to war. Impossible. He wouldn't believe it. He was a good ol' boy, he was. As good as gold. Soon as ever as he'd done his day's buyin', he'd be up the pub. Back he'd go hoom at half-past ten, drunk as a lord. Him and his wife used to live over here durin' the main fishin' seasons, but they'd go back to Germany in between times to avoid becomin' subject to income tax. All the German representatives used to do that because if they stayed over here for six months, I think it was, they became liable to pay British tax. They weren't a bad lot o' lads. I liked 'em.

"I remember one year when I was up in Anstruther, there was a heavy spring fishin' down here at Low'stoft. That'd be about 1935 or 36. Yeah, we were up in Anstruther, where the herrins were supposed to be at their peak, and we were havin' a very, very slack time. The boats were workin' out orf the Firth o' Forth and comin' in with only about four or five baskets o' fish, praps a couple o' cran. So what my firm done was send one o' the blokes back down to Low'stoft to klondyke these spring herrins. They were nearly all spents, but they bought 'em because there was such a shortage. Once they were boxed up, they were sent down to Harwich by rail and then shipped across to Altona. April time was always a thin time for herrins because the German trawlin' fleet hadn't really gone to work by then."

Towards the end of May the season in Fifeshire began to draw to a close, as far as klondyking was concerned. The Lowestoft men returned home then and were sometimes stood off for a week or two until the productive Shetland summer fishing started. This was the second most important time of year for the German export firms and the physical demands made upon the men were not a great deal behind those exerted by the East Anglian autumn voyage. Considerable quantities of herring were sent straight to Altona from Lerwick and the boxing up was often done down the holds of the various freighters.

"We used to work places in the north o' Scotland, like Fraserburgh and Peterhead, and we'd even go as far up as Wick. When we were workin' Wick, there might be a few herrins up at Scrabster or Thurso, so we'd git on the lorry, go buy 'em, and bring 'em back. Our main place up there, though, was Shetland. After we'd come hoom from Anstruther, we used to go away to Lerwick about the beginnin' or middle o' June. You went by rail as far as Aberdeen and then you'd catch the mail boat to Lerwick. One year we even went klondykin' at Stronsay, in the Orkneys. We lived in an ol' church there, but we weren't there very long because they shipped us across back to Lerwick. Orkney weren't really big enough for us; there weren't the quantity o' fish landed there.

"When we went away down to Shetland, we took all our gear with us, clothes and things. Each bloke had a box to put the stuff in and that'd be took to Low'stoft railway station with 'Passenger to Lerwick via Aberdeen' writ on it. You never saw that no more till you got down to Aberdeen, then you'd check it all over and hire a cart to take it down to the mail boat – the *St. Suniver* or *St. Ronald*, or one o' them. Cor, and dint the boys used to be seasick sometimes! There used to be some rough ol' passages goin' across what they called *The Roost*, out between Orkney and Shetland. One year, when we went across, the boat was full o' Scotch gals goin' over to the curin' stations. And that was a bloomin' bad voyage, that was. Cor, you've never seen anything like it! People spewin' up. And then, o' course, them boats carried cattle and sheep – well, they were makin' a row and the smell was comin' up from below. Pooh, crikey! I'll never forgit that trip.

"Up in the Shetlands you seemed to git different classes o' herrin'. There used to be some very good biguns when the boats were workin' orf Noss head, but when they got down to Fair Isle the fish were oily and greasy and had a black gut in 'em. Now, the Scotch curers dint want them and nor did the Germans – except as a last resort, when there was nothin' else. O' course, you got a lot o' dumpin' in Lerwick. That was a common thing there. There'd be too many herrins landed sometimes and the bottom would go out o the market. The boats used to go out o' the north entrance then, dump the catch and go back to sea to git some more. Praps they'd git a price for 'em the next time. Not if they were too oily, though, because they wouldn't keep. And not if they had that ol' black gut in 'em, because that blacked the meat o' the fish all the way down.

"That used to be very busy down at Lerwick, but the work was easier than in a lot o' places because you were klondykin' right on board the boat itself – you know, the boat what took the herrins to Altona. That'd anchor in the Brassy (Bressay) Sound and the drifters would come right up alongside and unload straight into it. Yeah, you'd be down in the hold and the herrin' would be handed down to yuh in baskets. There'd be one man a-shiftin' the boxes (the hold used to be full o' them, see), one puttin' the salt on the fish, one the ice, and one a-nailin' down. And you went on like that and gradually filled her up. The steamboats were about 700 or 800 ton and they'd carry a deck cargo, as well as what was down the two holds. Altona was the place where the bulk o' the herrin' went, though they did go to Bremerhaven as well.

"There used to be about 30 of us Low'stoft men workin' for the klondyke firms as regular labour, and three of us were with Figena. When the Germans worked Scotland and the Shetlands, they amalgamated. Each firm sent over two representatives from Germany and they formed a combine and all worked in together. A buyer used to be appointed, and a foreman packer, and they all worked in with each other. Cor, we dint half send some boxes over from Lerwick! Yeah, you used to git plenty o' overtime there. You'd work all night sometimes when there was late sales. See, the boats often used to land late in Lerwick and you had to wait for 'em to come in. One thing, though – you never had to make boxes up there. No, they used to come over from Hamburg on the *freshers* (you know, the steamboats), along o' the ice. On the mainland, both on the west side and the east, we used to have the boxes made up for us by a timber merchant because we never had the time to do it.

"Up there in Shetland, that generally used to be blowin' a gale. Yeah, even in the summer that was bloomin' cold and wet and windy. And yit I can remember one year (that mighta been 1938) when the weather was lovely – just like bein' on the Riviera. There was about 14 of us in the lodgins we had in Lerwick. That was a great big ramblin' ol' place, built when the Dutch fishermen and buyers used to go there in the 18th century. The man what owned it was a merchant seaman and he runned what they called a *flit-boat*. That was a little ol' Scotch *runtie* what'd been gutted out and had a motor put in, and that used to carry coal and things to the various little islands. Yeah, she'd go chug-chug-chuggin' along out o' the north entrance at Lerwick, Whalsay and Unst and them places. Or praps she'd run up to Sullom Voe. That was what they called flittin'.

"You always had a handline with yuh up there – a *ripper*. That was a lead with about five or six hooks on and you'd lower that down over the side o' the fresher while you were waitin' for the drifters to come to yuh. You dint even need bait up there, as long as the hooks were bright! You used to catch haddicks, small *tusks, coalies*, and you could sell them for a bit o' beer money. There was an ol' girl called Aggie Jones who had a little stall at the back o' the fish market in Lerwick and she'd buy 'em orf yuh. O' course, they had cod farms up there at that time o' day. They used to split the cod open, salt 'em and lay 'em out to dry. Then, when they were thoroughly dried out, they used to pack 'em together, belly to belly, and send 'em abroad. That was a Mediterranean trade – Spain, Italy, Greece, and places like that.

"The season up there used to end in August. The fish used to take orf and the German trawling fleet would be right inta their season then. The trawlers would put really heavy landins inta Altona and Hamburg and Lerwick would fade away. Finish – till next year. The trawled herrins weren't as good, but there was a demand for 'em to put in tins. When Lerwick closed, we used to go down to Fraserburgh and from there we'd work our way back down to Low'stoft. We'd stop for a few days in Scarborough and Grimsby and generally do like that. I liked that summer voyage and I liked the people. He ent a bad ol' boy, the Shetlander. I was talkin' to a feller not so long ago and he say, 'When was the last time you was at the Shetlands, Ernie?' I say, 'Cor! Years ago!' He say, 'Well, if you were to go to Lerwick now, you wouldn't recognise it. There's new houses everywhere and oil people by the hundred!' I don't think I'd want to see it like that, somehow."

The German vessel *Anna Rehder* lying on the seaward side of Lowestoft bridge in the 1920's. This was a favourite place for Klondyke trade freighters to load.

CHAPTER THREE

Trading In Herrings

'Oh, we left the home grounds in the month o' June,
And to canny Shields we soon was bearin'
With a hundred cran of the silver darlings
That we'd taken from the shoals of herring.'
(The Shoals Of Herring – Ewan MacColl)

One of the noticeable things about the fishing industry is the closeness of family ties. Time again the same surnames keep cropping up and there is quite often no difficulty in tracing back, on the strength of oral testimony alone, any one family's connection with fishing over three or four generations. The old, enforced (through there being very little alternative employment) stability of a particular way of life carried on into the modern period, by which time one might have expected it to have changed. The fact that it did not change says much about the pre-eminence of fishing and about the adaptability of the people involved who experienced great technical innovation during the late 19th and early 20th centuries, but who often exploited it to their own advantage. Some families used the new opportunities to rise in the social scale and enter into the world of business. Nor was this confined to those who lived in the two main fishing ports. To the north of Great Yarmouth lay Caister, to the south of Lowestoft was Kessingland, and in each of these villages lived a number of men who were among the more influential boat-owners in their respective neighbouring ports. Kessingland, in fact, was reckoned to be so wealthy in terms of its connections with herring fishing that, in the years leading up to the First World War, it was known as Klondyke. Local pride also designated it the richest village in the kingdom and, even after allowing for some natural exaggeration, it is clear that there was money in the place.

Evidence of the fact remains today, and is not hard to find. A number of substantial houses, which once belonged to boatowners, still survive. So do some of the net-stores, where the fishing gear was kept and serviced. Then there are the house names themselves, with maritime links such as Eddystone, Grassholm and The Knoll. It was in such residences that the ruling families of Kessingland lived: Catchpoles, Uttings, Manthorpes, Durrants, Strowgers and Gouldbys. These surnames are all in the minutes of the Lowestoft Mutual Fishing Vessel Insurance Co. Ltd's inaugural meeting held at the *King's Head*, Kessingland on Saturday, June 7th, 1862.

One of the men present was Edward Gouldby, grandfather of Clifford Gouldby (1889–1977), himself a fish merchant of long standing in Lowestoft.

"My grandfather started the firm round about 1860, I should think. And when the Herring Market was first built he had the first choice of an office there, and that's how our office came to be Number One, Herring Market. He lived at Kessingland, my grandfather did, and that was originally my home and all my family's home. Some of us moved to

Low'stoft later on, but Kessingland was where we came from. We owned several boats in our family and my father had both drifters and trawlers. The *Waveney* (LT 222) was one o' his and he was actually a director of the Waveney Steam Drift Fishing Company. Oh yes, he had various companies and different friends o' his were in business with him. The Garroods o' Beccles, who used to fit the boats with engines, they were in with him. I had boats myself and some o' them were partnerships. The *Peep o' Day* (LT 187) was; so was the *Our Friend* (LT 72). My father was secretary o' the Star Drift Fishing Company and that was yet another Kessingland concern. See, a lot o' the big owners came from Kessingland – more in proportion to its actual population, I should think, than came from Low'stoft.

"I used to keep my drifters' stores down on the Whapload Road, at Low'stoft, but my father had his net stores in Kessingland. I should think that him and his companies must have had about 50 or 60 beatsters working for 'em. We used to have a lot of horses as well and several o' them used to be stabled at Kessingland. They'd come down through town every morning, pulling the carts. Oh, it was nothing for them to do that. We had two-wheeled carts and four-wheeled ones, yuh know, and then the lorries started to appear some time before the First World War. I think we must have been among the first people in Low'stoft to have lorries."

Thus in a few words about his own family Clifford Gouldby sketches what is almost a potted history of the Lowestoft herring industry. Waveney Dock, to give the Herring Market its official name, was opened in 1881; the two fishing companies mentioned were among the first limited liability ventures to be formed locally; the Garrood family was one half of the famous firm of Elliott & Garrood, pioneers of marine engines, and the *Peep o' Day* was one of the first steam drifters to be built. Clifford himself was employed in the family business from a comparatively early age.

"I was away at Framlingham College till I was 16. Then, one day, I said to father, 'I think it's time I gave it up. I'd rather be working.' Now, my father was very good and allowed me to make decisions sometimes, so he took me at my word and I joined him. I went into his office on the Herring Market, along o' the two clerks he had, and started like that. Learning the business was partly forced work really, but I was interested in it. I don't think just anyone could pick it up – not without being interested. See, we were quite a big firm. We did kippers and bloaters and everything like that at our yard on Whapload Road, and we stored all our empty boxes and barrels there as well. Red herrins were another thing – we did an enormous quantity o' them. In fact, I suppose we were about the biggest firm for them in Low'stoft at one time.

"We had a list o' customers so big it would be ridiculous to mention 'em all. I mean, we had a big trade in East Anglia – Norfolk, Suffolk and Essex – but we also sent to places like Merthyr Tydfil. We had a strong connection with the South Coast, places like Hastings, Margate, Ramsgate, Dover and Brighton. Hastings was a very good customer trade, with about six shops chiefly for fresh herrings. We didn't push a great deal o' stuff down to London, though if we occasionally got left with any quantity o' fish we'd send it to Billingsgate. There were customers o' ours in Liverpool, Bristol, Sheffield, Leicester, Hull. Oh yes, all them places. With some that'd be on a regular basis (you know, they were retail firms), but with others what were in the wholesale trade you'd work on commission.

We had a tremendous big trade in Manchester. Tremendous! And all by rail. We had a firm there which went right back to my grandfather's time – Bain, Shorten & Co. Then there was another one where the man owned his own doss-house. That held about three or four hundred people and he imported herrins from us just for that.

"We were in klondyking as well. My father was in it with Walter Wood-Greaves. They had an agent over in Hamburg, because that was the place for the klondyke herrins in Germany. Well, it was Altona, actually – Altona, on the Elbe. I was never in it myself, not when I went into business on my own. But I used to send herrins over occasionally; you could always send, even if you weren't a member of the exporters' association. There were special steamers to carry the herrins over, all properly hired, and my father's firm even used to send over from North Shields. The herrins used to go over on the Newcastle steamers, because they ran on a direct service to Hamburg, and all the fish were packed in ice and salt.

"North Shields was one of our most important ports. The herrins there were very oily and, as a consequence, they used to burst in the belly. We had to select them very carefully. We used to have women selectors working over a sorting board before we sent 'em off to our customers. After North Shields was finished, towards the end o' the summer, we used to go down to Grimsby and work there. I remember bein' at North Shields one year (I was only 16) when everybody else had moved off to Grimsby. Yes, my father's buyer, Tom Sharman, and the other two men had gone down to open Grimsby on the Saturday and I was left alone up at North Shields. Well, as it turned out, Grimsby was blank (no herrin'), so I got a wire from my father sayin' 'Buy enough for 50 boxes.' They were for Germany, yuh see. Then I got another telegram – 'Buy enough for 100.' So I did as I was told. Then I got another one saying 'Buy all yuh can.' I had a helluva day (excuse me swearin'). See, all the herrins had to be packed in boxes, iced up and nailed down, and I was short-handed because the other men had left. Me and the woman who done the selectin' worked on our own right through the day, and we never even stopped for dinner. I just sent her over to the pub for a gallon o' beer and some eatables. When I got hoom at the end o' the season, my father say, 'I want to buy you a present for that day you had at North Shields, so you remember it.' I say, 'Oh, I shall remember it. I shall remember it all the days o' my life.' But, anyway, he was as good as his word and he bought me a twelve-bore shotgun, because I liked to go shooting.

"There was lot to see to in the fish trade in them days. Looking after the empties and getting them to where you wanted 'em was very important. See, you had different sizes o' box and all that. There was the margarine box, which held three stone o' fish, and then there was a larger case which held six stone. We had barrels as well and some of 'em held up to 40 stone o' fish. They were all for fresh herrin' for customers and you'd take them down to the boats for the fishermen to fill up. Then you or your man would stand there and watch 'em shoot the herrins in and salt and ice 'em. Yes, the fishermen did the work, but you'd gotta stand there and make sure that you were getting fair measure. The canning companies in Low'stoft used to buy their own herrins. A chap called Charlie Osborne used to buy for Morton's and then Maconochie's had their own buyer as well. With the buying you'd gotta remember so many things. The demand would depend on the supply o' fish and you had to know how to work on the weather. See, if the weather was bad and you got a short supply, you'd gotta git in and buy quick. Then, if there was a poor trade through too many herrins, you'd gotta buy just right to beat it. Once you'd bidded in the sale-ring and had your price accepted, you could take what you liked. That might be five cran, or ten cran, or even the boat's whole catch.

"I believe it was about 1920 when I approached my father about takin' over the herrin' side o' the business. He couldn't control it because he had to concentrate on other things. He was a big man in drifters and trawlers, and that took nearly all his time. When I asked him about takin' over, he offered me half the business; but I wanted to go on my own because, where there's two of yuh, you're never certain of always agreein' on things. In the end he let me do it and I bought the Whapload Road yard off him, as well as all the empties we had there. O' course, we had thousands o' empties, yuh see – boxes and barrels – and they were all in that yard. It was where the Birds Eye factory canteen now stands.

"I used to buy at Yarmouth as well as Low'stoft. Yes, I had all the different ports, yuh see. I either used to go myself or was represented by someone working on a commission basis. The autumn herrins here were the firmest, but some o' the Scotch ones were pretty good too. I wanted to go to Ireland one year, but my father advised me not to because there was trouble there at the time. There was a port on the east side o' Ireland and they used to run herrins across to the Isle o' Man to be kippered. Then the kippers used to be sent across to our mainland in England. One firm I used to buy for, the British & American Salmon Curing Company, did a lot o' bucklings. Yes, I was buyer for them and about three other firms, besides my own, and I got paid a commission according to whatever my turnover was.

"There was a lot o' variation in the price you paid for herrins. One year there'd be a tremendous big supply, so they'd come down to about eight or nine shillins (40 to 45p) a cran, or praps even less. I remember Harry Catchpole and one o' the Scotch curers from Peterhead getting up in the sale-ring here at Low'stoft one year and sayin' that no herrins should be sold for under five shillins (25p) a cran. But I don't think that came to anything. The trawl-fish side went through a bad time as well.

"As regards the herrin' trade, I went all over Britain. Yes, I've bought in every port in Scotland, I should think, and I had branches everywhere. I used to work all the English ports as well – North Shields, Scarborough, Grimsby. Grimsby used to be in September before Low'stoft got started, but that was never a very big fishing. The main season was the autumn one out here – October, November, December time, nearly up till Christmas. There was a spring fishing here at one time, too, and I used to buy them herrins because there was nothing else about. When I was young and working for my father, we opened Newlyn as a mackerel port, and by that I mean we went down there to trade. We all went down, the whole family, mother as well. That was quite a big thing, the mackerel fishing. A lot o' the local boats went round to the West'ard to do a season. Another thing we did was sprats. Oh, we bought a lot o' them. I used to go down to Kessingland beach and buy 'em off the longshoremen, and I carried on doing that when I left father and went on my own.

"Like I said, though, the *Hoom Fishing* was our most important time, and I used to buy over at Yarmouth as well as in Low'stoft. I don't know if you've heard o' Harry Sutton o' Yarmouth? Well, he was a fish curer over there, chiefly for the Mediterranean trade (*golden herrins* and that), and a big buyer as well. He was very good to me, because if ever I went over there he'd always let me have some fish. 'Hullo, Gouldby,' he'd say. 'What're you here for?' 'Ten cran o' herrin', Mr. Sutton,' I'd say. 'Right,' he'd say. 'Go down to such and such a boat, see my chaps down there, and tell 'em that I said you can have ten cran.' And that's the good man he was. Yes, there was give-and-take among certain people, but there was animosity and trouble among others. I had two buyers in Low'stoft who were pure enemies o' mine. They hated me because I was getting on well in the trade and they tried to do me harm.

"I was always ready to take a chance in the fish trade. That's like when I was down at Fraserburgh one year, buying, and I couldn't get any good herrins at all because one o' the big curers was taking everything. Well, I knew that dogfish don't sell in Scotland, but they do in England, so I bought them instead o' herrin'. The same with gurnets. They were used as crab and lobster bait by the longshore boats at Sheringham and Cromer, and I'd buy them when I could. I'd always have a go at somethin'."

Given all the ups and downs of the fish trade, the one thing a merchant needed was steady customers, not necessarily clients who bought large quantities, but ones whose demand for fish was regular and reliable. A number of small men who ordered predictably and consistently was worth more than one or two large firms that came in with big requests at irregular intervals. Obviously, if a reliable trade could be built up with the larger fish-processing companies, all well and good, but people in a more modest way of business often provided the security necessary for a merchant's success. This was particularly true of the retail outlets, and fishmongers' shops were a major source of regular income. So, too, were some of the city and big town wholesalers.

"I had customers all over the country, some goin' back to my grandfather's and father's time and others that I'd built up myself. I had one called Feltham, down at Luton, and I'd send him 70 to 100 boxes o' bloaters at a time. There was about five or six stone to the box and he'd sell them down in his part o' the world. They had to be good bloaters too. Probably not as good as you'd buy from a curer like Reggie Reynolds, but pretty decent. The same with kippers. I had a lot o' customers for them, especially in the Midlands – Nottingham, Leicester, Leeds, and places like that. With customers who wanted fresh herrins you were always after fulls, but for kippers it didn't matter. You could kipper spents if you wanted to and it worked out cheaper. Another thing I did was build up a big trade in roes. I used to send 'em down to Billingsgate, the hard ones and the *milches,* and you either sent 'em separate or mixed up together.

"I had an enormous trade in Norfolk and Suffolk – well, right down as far as Colchester. Norwich, King's Lynn, Swaffham, Cromer, Wells – I used to send to all them places. Ipswich, that was another one. Bungay. I dealt with a man called Revell there. I even had a customer at Forncett St. Peter, which was right a little village. Motor lorries were a big help to me. I used to send them down to the station with stuff for all over the place. There used to be a special early train leave about three o' clock in the morning for London and the South Coast and I'd use my lorries to catch that. They were a big help, too, when I was working Scotland. I used to send a driver down to Carlisle from, say, Fraserburgh with a load o' fish and he'd meet another lorry there come up from Low'stoft with empties on board. The drivers used to change over motors then, and one would bring the empties up to me and the other would take his load o' fish on to wherever he was going.

"I also had about five or six drifters at one time and I did fairly well with them too. I had good men sailing for me, which was very important. The skipper was the main thing, yuh see. Yes, you had to have good skippers, though there was a certain amount o' luck to the business as well. Some o' my boats were built at Richards and some by the Yarmouth firm o' Fellows. Chambers was another firm here in Low'stoft which built drifters and for years and years the fishing was good. Yes, the industry flourished. The crews were paid on a share, with the skipper getting one share and a quarter and an eighth. Then that went down in stages till you got to the cook, and he was on a half-share. Some o' the fishermen did well, yuh know – till the slump came. Fortunately for me, I got rid o' most o' my boats before things got really bad, but my father was ruined. He kept all his drifters and trawlers and went to the wall. I even bought one off him, just to help out.

"Another thing I was involved in was the salt trade. I was agent for Seddon & Sons o' Middlewich, Cheshire. I even went to their factory once to see the salt made. That was all pumped up from underground – you know, the brine – through great big pipes. Pumped up hot and the water evaporated off so the salt was left. When I was buying for the British & American Salmon Curing Company, there was a place next to their yard down on The Beach at Low'stoft where Walter Wood-Greaves had once tried to make salt. He didn't succeed, o' course, because the salt water in the North Sea was nothing near down to getting good salt out of. When I was working for Seddon's, the salt used to come by railway, about ten ton to a truck, and then I kept it at my own premises in barrels. People used to come and get it as they required and I can remember one year when I sold 1,500 tons at a shillin' (5p) a ton commission. Yes, I did well that year. I earnt £75."

Klondyking at Anstruther during the 1930s. Ernie Armes is seen here holding a shovel as two fishermen get ready to shoot a basket of herrings into the case. A building and courtyard next to this harbour now houses the Scottish Fisheries Museum which has preserved examples of the distinctive zulu and fifie fishing vessels.

CHAPTER FOUR

Gone West

'Unite and unite and let us all unite,
For Summer is a-comin' today.
And whither we are going, we will all unite
In the merry morning of May.'
('Padstow May Day Song' – traditional)

Among the voyages away from home undertaken by East Anglian fishing vessels during the second half of the 19th century was the annual migration to the Cornish port of Padstow during the early months of the year. This began in the 1890s, or possibly even earlier, and it was the sailing trawlers (or smacks, as they were known) which began the exodus, with the main quarry being soles. Large quantities of these valuable flatfish were to be had close to land on the relatively unexploited inshore grounds of Cornwall, from Port Isaac down to Newquay, and it was a fishing that quickly grew. The development of steam vessels at the end of the 19th century, and their increasingly rapid build-up in numbers during the first decade of the 20th, led to more and more vessels making the journey from Norfolk and Suffolk each year, until by the outbreak of the First World War a notable fleet used to assemble each season.

Of the two ports involved, it was always Lowestoft which supplied more boats, because after about 1900 the trawling industry in Great Yarmouth declined sharply. Padstow came to be a very useful off-shoot for the Suffolk port, as business was traditionally slack for the first three months of the year on the home market. This was partly due to the winter weather conditions and also to the poor quality of North Sea plaice (one of Lowestoft's staple catches), which were then in their spawning season. Before the outbreak of war in 1914 the steam boats involved were mainly herring drifters, some equipped with *beam trawls* (the same gear as used on board the smacks), but after the cessation of hostilities the *drifter-trawlers*, with their *otter gear*, became the dominant vessels. By the late 1920s and early 30s anything between about 50 and 70 of them used to congregate at Padstow each year, drawing in their wake shore personnel from the home ports. Arthur Evans (1901–1984) was a teenager when he first went there, in the company of his fish-merchant father, but the 1920s saw him visiting regularly on behalf of the family firm.

"The first year I ever went to Padstow was in 1916. I was still at school at the time (Clegg's College) and we all went down – father, mother and my sister. It was during the Easter holiday and the reason we went was that trade was absolutely deadly on the Low'stoft market – very poor landings, you know. We'd only been down there about three days when the Germans shelled Low'stoft from the sea, so we missed all that. Father went down on his own after that. He wasn't the first Low'stoft man to go down there, o' course. Some o' the local buyers had been doing that season for a while. He also gave Fleetwood a try one year, father did, because there used to be a terrific lot o' soles in Morecambe Bay at one time. But he never went any more after that. No, he said it was too easy there – not enough competition. Everybody was buying at one level, which isn't necessarily good for trade. It wasn't any good for my father either, because he loved a bit of competition.

'When we all went down to Padstow as a family that time, we stayed at Ye Olde Shippe hotel. It belonged to a man called Ding and he was a real character. He was as bald as I am now and about four inches shorter, so you know how tall he was! He used to carry the processional cross in church and I shall never forget the first Sunday night that we attended service. Old man Ding came down the aisle, carrying this cross and looking really angelic. Then, when he got dead level with me, he looked sideways and shut one eye. You know, winked. I burst out laughing in church; I just couldn't help it. Oh, he was a real character. We stayed down for May Day that year and, o' course, everybody used to go mad in Padstow on May Day. I think they still do. Yes, there's no work done on May Day. The ol' girls were out about six o' clock in the mornin' and the drums were banging away. Some o' the people turned up at Ding's place right early 'cause they knew they'd be all right for a few drinks out o' the window. Oh, it was a rare day!

"My father got to know George Pawlyn for the first time that year. He was a Plymouth man who bought in the various ports all over Devon and Cornwall, and he was the undisputed King o' Padstow. Well, o' course, my father wanted to make his mark on Padstow, being new there, so for the first couple or three days he tried to buy every sole in sight. I think he and George Pawlyn had a right old barney over it, though after they got things sorted out they became great pals. They were two of a kind, really – both very strong characters. See, my father was from London originally and he ran away from home when he was about 12 or 13 because he didn't want to work in the family furniture business. He went and got a job in Hills Restaurant, right near Billingsgate Market, and then became a porter on the market later. He worked for J. T. Clark and he eventually became one o' their buyers. That's how he first came up to Lowestoft, in about 1899, to represent them here. He started to go into business on his account then."

The Lancashire port of Fleetwood became more and more important in the economy of Lowestoft throughout the 1920s and 30s, with increasing numbers of boats basing themselves there for a summer trawling voyage. The pattern was for the drifter-trawlers to go from Padstow during the second half of May and prolong their activity for the next three months by working out of Milford Haven, then moving on to Fleetwood. At the end of the summer a number of them would return to Lowestoft to re-gear for the autumn herring voyage, but some stayed trawling on the west side all year. Those vessels that left Padstow and returned home at the end of the sole fishing were usually converted back to drift-netting and sent on the summer herring voyage to Shetland.

"I used to go down to Padstow round about the end o' January and I'd be there till the middle or end o' May. I stayed in digs for about three seasons, then I had a dispute with the landlady and went and stayed at the Metropol. That was the top hotel there, but I got accommodation pretty reasonably because it was out of the holiday season and I knew the proprietor. I went down after soles mainly, because things were absolutely deadly on the Low'stoft market during that early part o' the year. For a prime-fish buyer, that is. Yes, fish were scarce and the quality was poor, and even when I got back in May you had to wait a month to six weeks before things got back into full swing. The soles at Padstow were very, very large. Yes, if you bought a 200 pound (91 kilos) kit o' soles, you'd be lucky if you got 15 pounds o' half-pound soles in. I bought thousands and thousands and thousands o' pounds worth o' soles down there, and all at about sixpence or sevenpence (2½p) a pound. The smaller ones you could sell for a lot more, because they weren't so coarse.

"The boats would only be out about a day or two, catching them, you know. Yes, they'd often go out overnight and be back next day with a ton or two o' soles. And, like I say, they were practically all jumbos, at about sixpence a pound. Only the small ones made any real money when you sold 'em. You might get up to about three shillings (15p) a pound for them. We used to send the soles all over the country, but the main outlets were to wholesalers in the big cities – places like Birmingham, Manchester, Liverpool. I used to send a terrific lot to Liverpool for the shipping trade and I can remember one order I had was for 10,000 pounds – weight. Yes, weight. That was a shipping firm and it was a very big order for those days because there was no freezing them. No, everything was sold on the bone; there was no filleting at all. Everything went out by train from Padstow, even though the services weren't particularly good – only two or three trains a day. Another thing about the soles round there was that they were very, very rough and hard on the hands. I've seen Roy Beatton, who used to work for us, with his hands all bleeding at the end o' the day, just through handling and packing them. In the end, pads used to come at the tips o' the fingers. They built up as a kind o' protection.

"There were other kinds o' fish as well as soles, o' course, but not in the same quantity. You got quite a lot o' roker, the blond rays particularly, but we never handled a lot o' that. I used to get a share o' the blond roker, but what I bought didn't count against the real people in that line. They were lovely fish, though; very, very big. You never see anything round this way like them. There were lemon soles as well, a few, but they were mainly small. The whitings weren't bad. You got quite a few o' them at times – and pout whitings as well, which we don't see a great deal of round here. Then there would be quite a lot o' gurnards and the odd stuff like conger eel and ling. I don't think Padstow was all that much of a port until our boats started goin' round; it was just mainly little longshore craft. I think they used to look forward to the boats from Low'stoft and Yarmouth arriving because that set the place alight for three or four months. The sailing smacks weren't going round in my time, though. No, they were just before. I don't really remember them. Though during the First World War, o' course, there were a lot of 'em in Padstow. That first trip o' mine in 1916 doesn't really count; I was only there on holiday. I didn't start buying until the 1920s.

"I stopped going down to Padstow about 1934, I think. The port didn't finish; I did. I can't remember exactly when our boats stopped going, but I seem to remember it was after the Second World War. There was a sandbank down at Padstow, right across the harbour, and it was called the Doom Bar. Everyone used to curse about it, but once it had gone it was found to have been more or less the saviour o' Padstow because it had broken the run o' the tide. It disappeared with a change of wind and tide, I believe, never to return, and that caused a tremendous difference in the rise and fall o' the water in Padstow harbour. The boats started to get knocked about so much that they stopped going down. At least, that's what I was told. I last visited the place back in the 1960s and it was full o' summer visitors. I was walking across the square, when a tall chap passing me by suddenly stopped and pointed his finger down at me. 'Young Evans!' he said. 'My name's Williams.' He'd recognised me, you see. I looked at him and then I said, 'Well, you must be young Barry

Williams!' And that was who he was. His family were newsagents in Padstow and he was only a small boy when I was down there. He'd grown into a darn great chap, but he remembered me."

Arthur Evans found Padstow greatly changed from the place he remembered, but it was not alone. When the Padstow sole voyage died away in the immediate post-war period, the Lowestoft and Yarmouth fishing fleets were much reduced in number from the 1920s and 30s. Enemy action had taken a toll of vessels requisitioned for patrolling and minesweeping duties. Different patterns of fishing were emerging too, with more emphasis on the North Sea (for trawling as well as for drifting). Old grounds which had had a six year rest during hostilities now beckoned once more with promise of plenty. It was no longer quite the same world as that belonging to a young man nearly 30 years before, as he tried to break new ground on a Cornish fish market.

"I was about 21 when I started to buy at Padstow, and I really hit trouble there that first year. I introduced myself to the other buyers and they were all very pleasant, said they were pleased to meet me and all the rest. Then, when it came to the sales, they wouldn't let me get in. There were about 12 sales that first day, but every time I tried to put my *tally* on a kit o' soles (just one, yuh know – I wasn't being greedy) one o' the other buyers would come along and say he was sorry, but he needed that kit for an order. That went on all day. They were all very friendly and very sorry, and I hadn't bought a single sole! The next morning, instead o' putting my tally on the kits I wanted and trying to get a share that way, I started to bid at the auction. So did they, and they chased me up. They were all laughing when I took the first sale because they thought they'd filled me up at a dear price and could then buy the second sale at their own rate. But I bidded for that one as well, pushed it right up to the limit, and took it. They stopped laughing then because there were only going to be five sales that day, and I'd got two o' the five. Well, to cut a long story short, I bought the lot! Yeah, and the only person I let have any was ol' George Pawlyn. He told me what he wanted and I let him have 'em, see, because him and my father were pals.

"He didn't half get on to those buyers. Yes, he really let go! They were mostly from London and he really let 'em have it. 'You thought you were bloody clever, didn't you?' he said. 'You thought you'd got him beaten. Well, you hadn't,' he said. 'And even if you do manage to beat him, you'll only cause his father to come down here. Then you'll all be bloody sorry!' They were all in a huddle, these buyers, and they didn't like what he said one little bit. Anyway, the next day I went right through the market again and took the lot! George Pawlyn didn't mind, because he just came along again and took what he wanted. Oh, he'd let you buy a whole trip orf a boat and then come along and ask for most of it. Ha, ha, ha, ha, ha! I never minded, though. No, I never questioned it, because if I got in any trouble I could always go to him. And I was very, very pally with his son. They were good people and I never minded selling however many kits to them. After I'd gone through the market again on that third day, the other buyers all came along and agreed to let me have a proper share o' the fish. But they tried to give me the smallest one, until I said I'd go through the market again if I wasn't at the top o' the list. They gave in after that and treated me fairly, but it was murder for those first three or four days.

"When I went down, my father told me, 'If you get in trouble, you get out of it.' And that was what I was able to do, because I'd got a fair idea o' London prices in those days and I also knew about the little fiddles the buyers worked. See, the weights down in Padstow were very good. Yes, all the kits were well filled; everybody was happy. Now, the London buyers were paid a weekly wage by their firms, so any overweight that was going they sneaked for themselves. Oh yes, they had that and sold it for cash somewhere on the market. What overweight I got was going to my father. Oh, I soon weighed up what was going on, right from the moment I got there, and that's why I bought up all the sales those first two days. See, I wasn't just keeping them out o' the fish; I was hitting them right in the pocket as well.

"That really amused George Pawlyn. See, he was virtually the King o' Padstow, as I said, so he could afford to sit back. When I got down there that first season, his barrels were all over the market and there was hardly any room for anyone else. I went to the harbour master and asked for some working space and he refused. It took the threat of a phone call to his head office before he'd clear me a place to work in. They were such a big firm down there, you see, the Pawlyns were. They had a man in every little port in Cornwall, practically – even if it meant only buying crabs and lobsters. When Padstow opened up, they'd go there and they used to buy half as much as the rest o' the market put together. They were good people, though. Oh, I liked 'em. I used to go over to Plymouth for the weekend sometimes and they'd always take me back to Padstow in time for the Monday morning market. Yes, I had one or two rather good weekends over at Plymouth! See, that was the Pawlyns' home port. They did have a go at getting into the Low'stoft market at one time, but it never came to anything. A nice chap called Jimmy Beane bought for 'em, but it wasn't a great success. It's very difficult to get into a port sometimes, especially one that's going all year. See, there are all the established people to contend with.

"Yes, seasonal ports like Padstow were easier to open, though even there some chaps came unstuck. We had a feller come down one year from Fleetwood, about 1927 or 28 time, and he ought to have made a lot o' money. He was a war hero, they said, and quite a decent bloke as well, but he was silly with it. He came onto the market as if he was going to rule the roost, which is the wrong way to do things. It wasn't long before he'd upset nearly everyone and got shut out as a consequence. I felt sorry for him because he was such a hell of a worker. I've never seen a man who could wing *roker* like him. The speed! Yes, he'd pick 'em up and be through them twice with the knife – whack, whack. He could do a kit on his own in the time it took two men in the normal way. I've forgotten his name now, because it was so long ago, but I was really sorry about the way he got crowded out. He ought to have been earning God knows what with his ability."

The drifter-trawler *Arcady*. This steel-hulled vessel was built in 1910 and was typical of the kind of boat which went round to Padstow in the early months of the year to fish for soles. She is seen here without trawling gear.

CHAPTER FIVE

Selling The Catches

'Now up git the sole with his eyes on the side:
Says he to the skipper, 'Let me be your guide.'
In this windy ol' weather, boys, how the sea roar.
Stormy ol' weather, boys, how the sea roar.'
('Windy Old Weather' – traditional)

An important figure in the fishing industry is the selling agent, or fish salesman. Fish-selling companies are either independent operators or the offshoots of firms that own boats, and in each case they remain a powerful instrument in the financial structure of the industry. Their job is to get the best possible price for the fish landed, but since the Second World War, and particularly in the last ten to fifteen years, the old market forces of supply and demand have had less effect, due largely to much of the total catch being bought by big processing firms, whose regular requirements for large quantities of particular varieties of fish tends to be its own arbiter.

In earlier times fish salesmen were also often responsible for administering the day-to-day running of the fishing boats themselves, at least, where vessels were owned either by very small companies or by private individuals. This meant taking care of all supply and repair work, conferring with the skipper about which grounds would be fished, looking after crewing arrangements, and even writing letters home for fishermen who were illiterate. Like all middle-men, who earn their living by taking a commission on the work they do, fish-salesmen have tended to acquire a dubious reputation in the industry. No doubt there were those among them who were both unscrupulous and dishonest, but there were certainly others whose integrity was known and respected. Mitchell Brothers was a firm of long-standing on the Lowestoft market and one that was well liked. Harold Mitchell (1903–1985) was grandson of the founder and a man with over 50 years experience in the fish-trade.

"Mitchell Brothers was formed in 1898 by my grandfather, John Mitchell, and his brother Willie. I can't tell you exactly when my father, George Mitchell, joined the firm, but I should think it was fairly early on. I started when I left Framlingham College in 1919. The only staff we had down on the market was my father, my cousin Billy Brown (he was clerk and general factotum) and me. I just did a little book-keeping when I first began. See, when you sold a *shot* o' herrins, you issued the boat's hawseman with a cardboard docket which had the names o' the buyers on it and the quantities they wanted. There might be as many as five or six names; just occasionally there'd only be the one. Once the buyers had got their fish, they would sign the docket to say so and it would be returned to the office. When it came in, the figures had to be entered in the day-book. There was a column for the boat's name, a column for the buyers and columns for the quantities bought and the price. When all the figures were entered, you'd add up the boat's shot and put the total down. It might come to £98.10s, we'll say – well, that sum was then transferred to the boats ledger, where you kept a record of the earnings of all the boats you sold for. The buyers' sums were put in the buyers ledger and you also made out daily bills for what they'd bought. On a Saturday I used to add up all the bills and cousin Billy would go through the buyers ledger, and both o' them had got to agree. If you'd sold £1,000 worth o' fish for the week, your bills had to add up to that, so did the buyers ledger and so, o' course, did the individual boats' earnings in the boat ledger. Certainly. And then, on Monday mornings, you'd take the bills round to all the various people.

"When I first began selling, I started with longshore stuff. You know, herring and sprats. Father came with me, just to keep an eye on what was happening, and I think I did some *stocker bait* as well. That was fish from off the smacks and trawlers (things like gurnards and weevers) which was sold as part o' the crews' earnings. It didn't make very much money, but I can remember the first lot I sold pretty well. I was a bit on the nervous side and I wished the ground would open! See, I was only 16 when I left Framlingham College, and I was 21 when I first went round to Plymouth, so that was somewhere between those two ages when I sold my first lot o' fish. I went to Plymouth in the December o' 1924. Father decided to open the port because we had about half-a-dozen boats we could sell for and he sent me round to represent Mitchell Brothers. Those six boats did well, too. I think they nearly all grossed £1,000 or more, which was a lot o' money in those days. We had more boats to sell for in the following seven or eight years that I went, but they didn't do as well as that first season.

"The voyage took place during December and January. There wasn't much doing in the herrin' line in Low'stoft then, so several o' the boats used to go to Plymouth. It wasn't very far from port out to the fishing grounds round there and there were some good herrins to be caught out on The Ritz. Three boats which always seemed to do well were the *Dick Whittington* (LT 61) – skipper, Alec Penman; the *Girl Margaret* (LT 420) – skipper, Tiny Turrell; and the *Buckler* (LT 756) – skipper, Silvery Thompson. I didn't sell for them, though, because they were all in other offices. We used to sell on Christmas Day, if necessary, but I can only remember one occasion where I did any good. That was the year the Germans sent some trawlers down for klondyke fish and they anchored out in the Sound. Yes, one of our boats got a fair shot that particular time. There weren't too many skippers that went to sea on Christmas Day, o' course, but one or two did. I didn't get my Christmas dinner that year till about five o' clock because I had to wait for the docket to come back from the boat. The wife was with me then. We were staying in a furnished flat. See, after we got married in the April o' 1926, she used to go with me on the voyages away from home.

"Apart from that year when the German trawlers came, the Plymouth herrins were mainly bought by London buyers representing the Billingsgate firms. They were good herrins, too – especially for the time o' year when there wasn't a great deal of stuff about. You used to get several urchins down on the market after fish because the Barbican was in a poor neighbourhood. Yes, there'd be a lot o' little boys with their trousers all out and they'd go and sit on the kits o' herrin' and try to steal a few. They'd put their hands in, grab hold o' half-a-dozen and take 'em down to the other end o' the market. 'Who'll give me thrippence for 'em?' they'd say. And some o' the small buyers would take them. O' course, they knew what the boys had done, but there you are – herrins were herrins.

"At the end o' that season I used to come home for a few weeks and then go away to Newlyn about the beginning o' March for the mackerel fishing. I did that every year until 1940.

"Shetland was another regular place I went to. Yes, I first visited Lerwick in 1924 and went down every year until 1939. I remember one season there in the 1920s when one of our boats came in at four o' clock in the afternoon with 100 crans on board. I'd had advance news of this from one o' the other boats and I knew that the shot wouldn't be much good because at the time I got the message, just after dinner, herrins were already down to five shillings (25p) a cran. Now there was a man there called Ernie Cooper, who my father had asked to keep an eye on me, and I told him about these herrins. He suggested that we go to see a curer named Joe Mair, which we did. This Joe Mair had been a good friend of my great-uncle Willie and he told me to put the herrins up in the sale-ring and he would give me five shillings a cran for them. 'If you can git 5s. 6d. (27½p) for 'em, let 'em go,' he said, 'because I don't really want 'em.' Then he said, 'I'm only doing this for your Uncle Willie, you know, because he was a great friend o' mine and an honest and upright man.'

"There used to be hundreds and hundreds of crans dumped at Lerwick. Yeah, the boats would go out o' the north entrance, dump the catches, and go to sea and catch some more. The market had gone, you see. The curers could only handle a certain quantity because their girls could only gut a particular amount in a certain time. As long as the supply was just sufficient, or a bit under, the market was steady or rising. But if the buyers could get twice as many herrins as what their staff could handle, the price used to come right down. There was one particular year, though, when there were no herrins at all in Lerwick. That was 1939.

"A lot o' the boats left Lerwick and went over to the west side o' Scotland. They didn't have the right nets because a bigger mesh was needed round there (about 28 to 30 rows to the yard, I think), but the skippers decided to give it a go. There were big herrins down that way – Stornoway, Castlebay, Mallaig, Oban – but I alway stuck to Lerwick. It used to be a very busy season in Shetland. I should say 75 percent o' the Low'stoft drifter fleet used to go there, so you got quite a contingent o' local boats workin' Lerwick. When the spents began to set in, in August, the fishing closed and the boats gradually worked their way back home – Wick, Fraserburgh, Peterhead, Scarborough, Grimsby, right the way back to Low'stoft. We used to like to get home for Regatta Day, which was the last Thursday in August; then the boats would start off again on the North Sea, before the Home Fishing set in properly. They used to fish the Dowsing Ground, but some owners never allowed their craft to go down there because the herrins were all *maisy* and there wasn't a sufficient depth o' water for the nets to float properly. Those that did have boats fishing there usually sent 'em down with old nets specially kept for the purpose, so it didn't matter whether they got lost or not.

"I never went down to Lerwick after the war. No, there wasn't the number of boats to go down for. Before the war, when the boats were working back down the coast to Low'stoft, we used to have a representative in all the various ports who would sell for our boats if I wasn't there myself. I forget the names of all the firms now, except for J. Graham & Sons at Hartlepool, but there'd be someone to represent us in the different places. My three ports away from home took up eight months o' the year. December and January I was in Plymouth; March, April and May, Newlyn; June, July and August, Lerwick. Then, after that lot, I did the Home Fishing, which would take me up to the Plymouth voyage again."

While away from home, the fish salesman had a number of other duties to perform in addition to his auctioneering, the most important of which was attending to the needs of the vessels whose catches he handled. A smoothly run and happy ship was reckoned a big factor in its financial success.

"While you were away from home, you were agents for everything. I mean, if a boat was making water, you had to get her on the slip for repairs. Then, if there was a collision with another boat, there'd be a statement to take orf the skipper and the insurance to sort out. When I was down in Lerwick, I used to see to getting the nets mended. I got *beatsters* for that wherever I could and then I'd see that the nets were laid out on the fields and dried. I helped to lay 'em out and take 'em up many a time. The only thing I didn't have anything to do with was coalin' the boat. No, that was always taken care of by the skipper and the coal companies. The local firms here, Craske, Bessey & Palmer and the Lowestoft Coaling Company, used to have coal hulks down at Lerwick. Steamers would come and empty the coal into these hulks and then the drifters would go up alongside and take on what they wanted. It was easier, really, than getting coal in Low'stoft because it had to be brought to the boats here in little wherries.

"Another thing I did when I was away from home was act as *ship's husband*. Sometimes there'd be crewin' problems. You might get a man with poisoned fingers, so you'd go into the fishermen's mission then and try to get a nightman. That would be a local man most likely, and you'd pay him so much a night and a share o' the catch according to his position on the boat. Occasionally, you'd have a man who was no good, so you'd have to sack him and send him home. Then you'd hope that they could find someone in Low'stoft to replace him. It was very, very difficult to get good men in the 1930s because, naturally enough, the best fishermen went with the best skippers. Those skippers who didn't earn a lot o' money – well, they just had to take who they could git. There must have been a lot o' luck in herrin' catching, but it can't have been all luck. No, I think certain skippers were praps a little bit more brainy and took notice of things. It's like those three I mentioned earlier, who used to go to Plymouth. If anyone had herrins, they did.

"The Home Fishing was always busy. Yes, it was – even in the 1930s, when things were not very good at all. And, in spite o' things being bad, I don't remember any dumped herrins here in Low'stoft – not like there was in Lerwick. No, there always seemed to be an outlet somehow or other. They often went very cheap, o' course. Yes, if you had a hundred cran shot and got a £1 a cran for 'em, that was considered good. I suppose it was a toss-up between the klondykers and the Scotch curers as to who bought the most, but there used to be a terrific lot o' herrin' also sold to what we called freshers. They used to buy the fresh herrins for kippering and all that sort o' thing. A lot of 'em had vats as well, just the same as Sutton and all the Yarmouth firms did, and they'd buy lots o' herrins when they were cheap and put 'em down in the vats.

"Everything was sold by auction. Yes, we'd start off at a certain price (ten bob, we'll say) and then go upwards till the highest bidder took the herrins. It wasn't necessary that one buyer take the whole shot, though. No. Sometimes there'd be half-a-dozen or even ten people all take what quantity they wanted. That meant you kept puttin' 'em up for sale each time and getting a slightly lower price as you went along. The other thing was that prices did tend to go down as the day went on. If you were lucky enough to have a boat come in at nine o' clock in the morning, you'd probably git £1 a cran. But the price would be down to 15 bob (75p) by 12 o' clock. That was just the way it went. Sometimes the market would go up, but not very often. No, it was usually down. The Scotch curers used to take advantage o' that to find fault with the sample and chuck the catch up. See, they realised that the price had dropped down from the time they had bought the herrins, so they'd reject the sample and get a re-sale. And that meant they'd get the herrins cheaper next time round. It caused a lot o' bad feelin', that sort o' thing, so the Herring Industry Board eventually stepped in and appointed an arbitrator to sort things out.

"Even very small buyers could be in a sale, if they liked. Yes, I mean someone like Stanley Gibbs would come and buy praps a couple o' cran. Anybody was allowed to go and buy herrin', provided they could pay for 'em. We used to give weekly credit. And there was a fish salesmen's meeting every week to discuss how things were going down on the market. The Home Fishing was a two month thing really, with October and November being the busiest time and with trade quietening down in December. A big improvement that came in before the war was the use of tins to land the catches in. I don't know who first started it, but I think it was Jack Breach. There were six tins to the cran and they were made o' aluminium. With using them, a boat could leave its catch on the quayside and put out to sea again, where with the old way of having the herrin' loose down the hold a boat had to wait until the sample had been auctioned in the sale-ring and the fish unloaded in baskets. Oh, using tins saved time. That it did.

"O' course, the gold-rush in the herrin' trade was between about 1895 and the start o' the First World War. Yes, I've heard my father say that the boats were paying about 20 percent profit on the investment made and the banks were running after people just to lend money to 'em. Something like 1,000 boats used to gather in Yarmouth and there was a good lot here in Low'stoft as well. That all changed durin' the 1920s and 30s, though. Yes, the trade dropped right away and controlled fishing was introduced to try to regulate the market. The Ministry stepped in and wouldn't allow the boats to go out on a Saturday night (this was in the 1930s). Before they did that, you never started to balance up your week's bills till about six o'clock on a Saturday evening because you never knew if a boat was going to come in and land late. I mean, I have gone home at about one or two o' clock in the small hours o' Sunday morning. Not often, I agree; but it did happen. After the war pooling was introduced, whereby all boats that landed up to a certain time went into a particular pool and got an average price for their herrins. The salesmen had to send all their figures into the pooling office in Suffolk Road and the men there would work out the price."

Up till now the emphasis has been very much on the sale of herrings caught by steam drifters, because it was herrings which constituted the bulk of Mitchell Brothers business. Various members of the family also owned boats in their own individual names; and while these vessels provided the foundation for the selling venture, there were other boat owning firms whose catches were also handled. Another side to the whole enterprise was the conducting of trawl-fish sales. This became increasingly important in Lowestoft after the Second World War, particularly when North Sea herring catches began to diminish during the 1950s and the Home Voyage eventually came to an end round about 1967/68, Lowestoft had been a trawling port of some note ever since Kentish fishermen from Ramsgate had arrived and settled there in the 1860s, and an established white-fish industry helped to offset some of the worst effects caused by the decline of herring-catching.

"Besides our own boats, we sold for some o' Arthur Gouldby's and one or two other firms as well. Our commission for doing that was five percent o' the value o' the catch, but it wasn't always stuck to. No, you'd give a rebate of something like 1¼ to 1½ percent in order to get the business. I can't tell you what the figure was exactly because those arrangements were made by my father. You had to try to git the best price you could for the boats whose catches you were sellin', o' course. Yes, because if you didn't the owner would want to know why. That was just the same with trawl-fish, though I never actually sold any trawl-fish apart from here at Low'stoft. I think the firm o' Tom Richards sold for our boats down at Padstow and the Low'stoft Fish Selling Company round at Fleetwood. Then there was a cousin o' my father's at Milford Haven, Arthur Mitchell, who worked for us and had a house built in the place. He even started up a coalin' business on his own and went into a shipchandlin' business with a man by the name o' Kerr. As the herrin' gradually died out after the Second World War, we went into more trawling. Yes, our boats used to work out here in the North Sea. The catches were sold by auction just the same as herrins, but all the fish were packed into *trunks* and kits before the sales started.

"We had boats trawling before the war as well. Yes, we had the *Glen Heather* (LT 62) and the *George Baker* (LT1253) – and then, o' course, after the war we had the *Cairo* (LT 154), which Ned Mullender was skipper of for a time. We even had a bit of an interest in smacks at one time (this was before the war) because we sold for a firm by the name o' Painter, which owned smacks. One o' their boats was called the *Lent Lily* (LT 486) and another one was the *Thyme* (LT1222), skippered by a man by the name o' Harry Pendle. She was one o' the first smacks to have a motor put in her, I think, and the work was done by Richards, the shipbuilders. Or, at least, they supplied the engine.

"Another thing we did was run a salt store. Nearly every fish salesman ran salt down on the quay, just up-through-bridge past the Customs House. There was quite a lot o' salt used by the drifters, and when they went away on a voyage, they'd praps take a ton or two with 'em. They used the salt for overdays mainly, but they'd sprinkle the nets with it sometimes after a big shot. Yes, when they were pulling the nets down and cleaning 'em after they'd landed, they'd put salt on to kill the oil from the herrins. See, they were cotton nets then and they tended to heat up. As far as I can remember, I don't think my father ever *netted* any boats. No, he didn't believe in it, because he said that the man who owned the boat wouldn't care about how the gear was looked after. It didn't belong to him, so why should he worry about it?

"The net stores we had didn't belong to Mitchell Brothers. No. They were the individual stores belonging to the different boats. See, Mitchell Brothers was pure and simply a fish salesman's concern. Different members o' the family owned boats or had shares in 'em, but as private individuals only.

"Back before the war I should think we handled about 75 percent o' the longshore business. Nowadays they call these 70-footers longshore boats, but they're not really. They're inshore craft, which to my idea is entirely different. You can't work 'em orf the beach. The biggest longshore boat before the war was Jack Swan's *Surprise* and I think she was about 25 or 26 feet long. You see, you'd only git praps four or five stone (25.4 to 31.75 kilos) o' fish to sell for each boat. That'd be shrimps or trawl-fish in the summertime and herrins in the autumn. Some people used to go after the spring herrins as well, but not in such numbers. Oh, there was a living in longshoring, but it was very small money. A lot o' boats used to be involved. I mean, it wasn't just Low'stoft. There was Pakefield, Kessingland, Southwold, Aldeburgh, all the way along. During the Second World War the November sprat season suddenly dropped right away after about a couple o' years, and it never came back. I don't know why, but that's what happened. It forced the Aldeburgh people to find another living and that's why they went into longlining for cod.

"The longshore stuff was smaller than our main business, but we sold on a commission basis just the same. Yes, I sold longshore herrins for the whole o' the 55 years I was in the trade. The fish from away used to come down to the market in lorries, vans, private cars, anything. The latter part o' the time we were sellin' stuff from King's Lynn down to Southend – crabs, roker, herrins, sprats. We weren't the only firm, o' course, and the supply varied a good deal, but we did cover that area. Before the war a lot o' the sprats caught out here went for smoking. F. H. Phillips and Harry Catchpole used to send them across to Ostend. Prices were very low in those days. I mean, I've sold shrimps from Kessingland at a shillin' (5p) a peck – all steaming hot! *Slips* were only thrippence (1½p) or fourpence (2p) a pound. You just can't realise it nowadays. When I finally finished down on the market, the Inshore Merchants Federation presented me with a Swiss pocket watch as a retirement gift."

The token of esteem was well-deserved and there had also been an earlier acknowledgement of Harold Mitchell's contribution to the Lowestoft fishing industry. When the rationing of fish came to an end in the post-war years (or, to be specific, when the period of restricted sales on the market ended), the Lowestoft Fish Merchants Association held a dinner to mark the end of wartime contingencies and, in particular, to record their appreciation of the exemplary way in which Mr. Mitchell had carried out his duties as Allocation Officer for Fish. They too presented him with a watch.

"When the Second World War broke out, the authorities eventually closed the Waveney Dock and the Hamilton Dock for fishing (The Navy took them over), and any o' the big boats that hadn't been called up for war service went to Fleetwood. There was only longshore boats left in Low'stoft when I came back from the Isle o' Man in the September o' 1940 and the only other sellin' firm was the Breeze Company. Everybody else had gone to Fleetwood. We carried on in the odd Trawl Market and I got appointed Allocation Officer through George Atkinson. He was the Ministry of Agriculture and Fisheries Inspector and he wrote to somebody in London and recommended me for the job. He said that as I was sellin' nearly all the fish, I might as well do the other job as well. Once I'd been appointed, nobody could sell any fish in Low'stoft without goin' through me. They got the commission on what they sold, o' course, but they had to come to me first. Durin' the war the position was honorary, because I wouldn't take any money. I'd got a brother fightin' in the forces and so I didn't think it right to be paid. After the war I got half-a-crown (12½p) per vessel and it was the boats themselves which had to pay.

"The idea o' havin' an allocation officer was to make sure that everybody got a fair share. See, fish was scarce; there were only longshore boats workin'. But, o' course, every little counted. The government fixed the prices for the different kinds o' fish and they also fixed the allocation allowed to each buyer. They worked it out on pre-war quantities, though I don't know exactly how they got the figures. There was an allocation for sprats, an allocation for herrins and an allocation for trawl-fish. In fact, there were about four or five different allocations o' trawl-fish to cover the different varieties – cod, plaice, etc. What I had to do was call out the different buyers names in threes, on each sale, and if any of 'em refused to take up their allocation the salesman could sell that fish to who he liked. Mind you, it wasn't very often that they refused! I had a book for each o' the different kinds o' fish and I had all the different buyers names in that, together with what they were allowed. It was a daily allocation and it continued in existence for about two or three years after the war as well. That had to be done because there was still a scarcity o' fish. I know the big boats came back from Fleetwood and out o' the war, but that was a gradual process and there was a lot more buyers about. You couldn't have people runnin' up prices all over the place and so they kept the allocation goin' for a certain period o' time."

The East Anglian boats returned to work in 1946 and '47 in what was still essentially an era of steam propulsion, but the change-over to diesel engines, started slowly in the 1930's, began to accelerate during the next decade and by the early 60's steam was very largely a thing of the past. Refrigeration played an increasingly important part, during the same period, as a means of handling and processing catches on shore, but in the case of the herring there came the time when there was nothing to handle. The Home Fishing died out in the mid to late 1960s and herring catching has never come back to Lowestoft on any scale – not even since the North Sea ban on taking the species was lifted in 1982. Morover, it is ironic that, while stocks may have now recovered, there is no real demand for catches.

"I suppose the main thing in my time is that the herrins disappeared. People used to think that herrins were inexhaustible, but the North Sea is only like a big pond and there's no doubt that it was overfished – especially by purse-seiners and trawlers. I mean, the drift net would let small herrins through the meshes, but purse-seines and trawls catch biguns and littluns alike. I don't know whether pollution is a factor. It could be. You think of all the filth that's emptied into the sea every day. When I was a boy you used to see umpteen jellyfish swimming about in Low'stoft harbour, but you don't see 'em now – the water's absolutely putrid. Trawl-fish is another thing. The catches there have gone down. At one time the boats could go down Dover way and git loads o' turbot and brill and one thing and another. They can't do it now. See, the boats have got more powerful and that gives 'em more catching-power. At one time, when sail was all there was, the sea produced more fish than was caught. Now it's the other way round – we're catchin' more fish than the sea can produce. At least, that's the way I see it.

"Another thing which made a lot o' difference in the trade was refrigeration. Before it came in, there was only salt and ice as the means of preservin' fish, but after freezin' was introduced you could keep fish a lot longer. You could also buy a lot when it was cheap, keep it in store and sell it gradually as the price went up. The first person to go in for that (this would be before the war, I think) was a man by the name o' Robinson. He started up what later became the Low'stoft Cold Store and he was laughed at by quite a considerable number o' people in the fish trade, both buyers and boatowners. The idea he had was to buy herrins when they were cheap and sell 'em when they went up in price, so his brains were better than a lot o' other people's. He could see ten or twenty years ahead and now, o' course, there's cold-stores all over Britain. After the war there was the Explorator firm with their insulated fish-lorries. They used to take herrins from Low'stoft to different places down south, but they were still usin' ice.

"Nowadays there's a lot o' imported fish comin' into Low'stoft from the Continent. It's brought in by container lorries and there's no doubt that it's had a bad effect locally – especially the Dutch plaice. O' course, there has been talk o' the different foreign governments subsidisin' their boats, but I don't know whether that's true or not. What I do know is that if you're a buyer you're not goin' to pay the local price for a kit o' fish if you can git it a good bit cheaper. There's nothin' wrong with the Continental fish; it's good quality. But, there you are, I couldn't see from the start where joinin' the Common Market was goin' to be any good to the fish-trade. I think that the people in favour of it were thinking more of things like the car industry, or praps agriculture, than they were of fishin'. I suppose the fish-trade was just a flea bite compared to those. No doubt they were very clever people who worked it all out, with a lot better brains than mine, but I don't think that they were all that bothered about the fishin' industry."

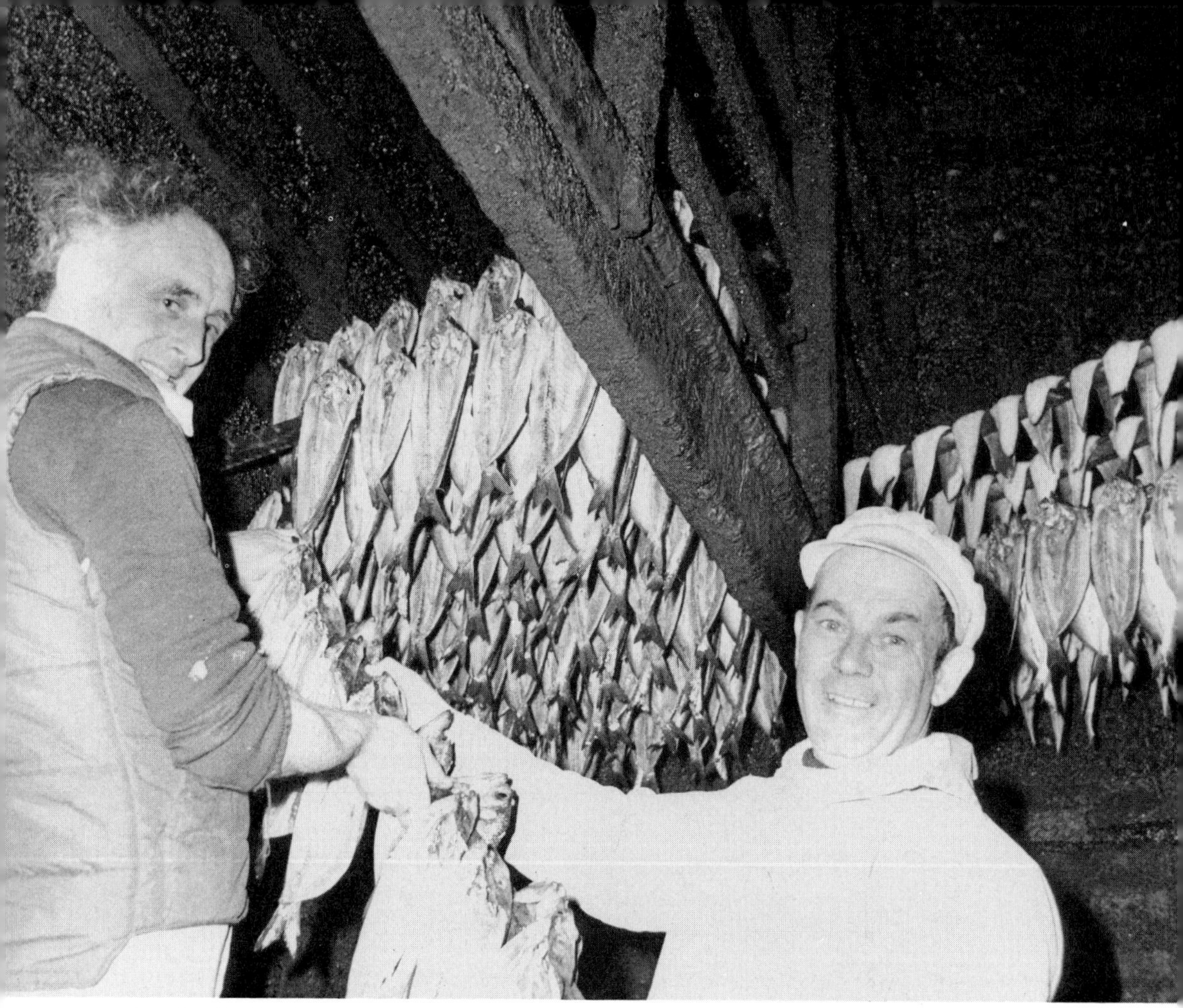

Gordon Buckenham and David Mullender, present proprietors of Reggie Reynolds's old smokehouse, seen hanging herring ready to start the curing process that turns them into kippers. (Photo. Rick Turrell)

CHAPTER SIX

Salt And Smoke

'What have I made of my old herring's guts?
Forty bright women and fifty bright sluts –
Wanton sluts and everything.
Do you think I've done well with my jolly herring?'
('The Red Herring' – traditional)

Before ice was used on any significant scale as a means of preserving fish (mid 19th century and onwards), the traditional methods were salting and smoking. Medieval wills of the 15th and early 16th centuries make specific reference to bequests of oak billets and salt being handed down from father to son, and there is no doubt that these merchants were involved in curing what later became known as *silver* and *golden* herrings. The dwelling-houses of such people stood at the top of the clay cliffs that overlook the sea, while down on the shingly denes below (at the bottom of the gardens, quite literally) were the net-stores and fish-houses – a basic topography which can still be seen today, although the surface appearance of the remaining buildings is largely 18th and 19th century.

After the arrival of the railway and the development of the harbour in the mid 19th century, the fishing industry in Lowestoft expanded rapidly and ancillary buildings sprang up all over town. Smokehouses were especially numerous and varied in size from the large commercial buildings (perhaps 50–60 ft length, 12 ft width and 25 ft height to the gable top) to the small backyard types (typically 9 ft × 6 × 10 ft), which were intended to serve the needs of the family in whose gardens they stood and produce a surplus for sale in the immediate neighbourhood. Most of them were built of brick (or of brick and flint-cobbles), with pantile roofs, and their rectangular and somewhat narrow appearance was determined by the way that the herrings were hung up on wooden rods, with these latter resting on racks fixed all the way up the walls from about head height. Smoke louvres, with adjustable wooden shutters, were inserted high up in the two long walls and there were sometimes flue-holes in the coping of the ridge itself. Only three such buildings remain at work in Lowestoft today and Reggie Reynolds (born 1906) spent a considerable part of his working life in one of them.

"My father's family lived down on The Beach in a road called *The Smile*. There was 19 children in the fam'ly and they had the only cottage with a cookin' stove out o' the whole row o' eight houses. Everybody else had to take their dinners down to old Gray the baker on Whapload Road to have 'em cooked. I've heard my father say how they used to lay head and tail in bed, and then one o' the older brothers would come in from sea and one o' the littluns would wake up with a pair o' dirty feet in his mouth! The kids used to have to go to Devereux's grocery shop, up on the High Street, with a linen basket and fill that up with bread what the mice had been eatin'. And another thing they used to do was go to ol' Ben Saunders's butcher's shop, at the top o' Rant Score and fill up a bucket with all the scrag ends o' meat. And that's what they used to live on. They were damn gret blokes as well in my father's fam'ly. Well over six foot, a lot of 'em.

"My father actually started work with his oldest brother, Jimmy, at the fish-house Jimmy had in Raglan Street. He used to drive the pony and cart down to the market, take stuff to the railway sidings to put it on the fish-trains to London. Then, when he came back, he had to stand at the bench and split herrins and *prick* on, as well as go up the loves and hang the fish. He used to start at half-past four in the mornin' and sometimes, when they were busy, he dint finish till ten at night! Imagine that six days a week for 18 bob (90p)! He used to have to see to the pony as well, groom and feed that, water it and bed it down. And he used to do the book-work, because his brother couldn't read nor write. Jimmy would come to him with a paper that had all strokes and crosses on it, and my father used to put it all down in the book. Mind yuh, there weren't no cheques to write out in them days; everything was done by cash.

"Eventually, my father started in business on his own. He took a smokehouse in Stanley Street, where the garage now is. It was a double-roof one, and we used to have kippers and bloaters one side and haddicks and cod the other. It was a bit of a conjurin' job to git them all in just right, but we managed. When I was a kid, I used to go there before school in the mornin' and as soon as I got out in the afternoon, makin' kipper boxes. I used to speet the bloaters up too; I'd stand outside doin' that, winter and summer. Sometimes I used to stand there and howl like hell when I was too cold. My father used to say, 'Clap your hands, boy!' Blast, I was only about eight year old when he got me on to splitting. I used to hefta stand on a box. 'Mind you dun't cut yourself, boy!' he'd say.

"When I left school at 13, I went cook three or four year on the smacks and the drifters. Then I had about another four year buyin' herrin' on me own. I used to go down to Scotland and send stuff back to my father, because he was in business with his brother Dick by this time. Yes, I used to feel the herrins over to see if they'd travel all right, then I'd buy what I wanted. I used to put 'em in boxes, ice 'em top and bottom, nail 'em down, then take 'em to the railway goods yard. I'd had a bit of experience o' buyin', yuh see. Yes, I used to buy longshores on the market here for my father and take 'em back home on the front o' the bike. Yeah, half a cran o' herrin at a time on the front of a trade bike! Then I'd take 'em back down onto the market again when they were kippered, because we had several customers for 'em down there. I have taken as many as 28 one-stone boxes o' kippers on the front o' that bike. When the policeman saw me comin' round Suffolk Corner, he used to stop all the traffic and let me through! Well, I could never have pulled up, not with that lot on the front!

"When I finished travellin' about, I went back in with my father and my uncle and I carried on with them till the war came on and buggered things up. I was in the forces for five or six year, then I got demobbed and gradually took the business over myself. See, my father and uncle were both gettin' old. Then, when my father died and my uncle packed up, I took the lot over completely. Back before the war, when my Uncle Jimmy died, my father bought his fish-house in Raglan Street and my Uncle Dick went and lived in the house so he could do the night smokin'. That became our main place, o' course, and I spent most o' my time in business on me own there. My wife used to help me a lot. Yeah, she used to do most o' the servin o' customers and she used to help with the prickin' on as well.

I could never git her to split, though. No. Mind yuh, that is awkward if you've got to keep stoppin' to go and serve people.

"The Shetland herrins were so full of oil that they used to split open. The ones from North Shields were just the same. If you didn't get really fresh Shields herrin', you could bet your bottom dollar that by the time they got to Low'stoft they'd be all busted open in the belly. They had a sort of a red gut in 'em as well, but they were marvellous to eat. Yes, they made the best kippers. I don't think there's anything eat better than a Shields herrin'. I reckon next to that is the Loch Fyne. I have heard some people say the longshore, but a longshore kipper is always on the dry side – unless you git a very exceptional one, and they're few and far between. Mind yuh, there used to be some nice longshores from Southwold and different places down the coast come onto the market the latter part o' the time I was in business, but the main herrin' voyage was dead and gone by then anyway. I only ever bought one lot o' Mersea herrin' and they turned out such bloody muck that I thought to myself, 'Reggie boy, that's the first and that's the last.' They're a freshwater herrin', see – caught up the Blackwater and places like that. You ought to ha' seen the *culch* that came out o' their guts! Oh dear, oh dear.

"We used to git some nice South Coast herrins up here about Christmas time. Then, as soon as they'd finished, there'd be the imported Norwegian herrin'. After them would come the local spring herrins and then you'd go onto the ones from Shetland and Scotland. The boats used to work all the way down – Lerwick, Fraserburgh, Peterhead – right back to Low'stoft for the Home Fishin'. If the herrins set in well, some o' the boats would work practically up till Christmas. They kept goin' further and further south till they were down at Cape Gris Nez. You used to git some good herrins at times from The Cape, but you also got a lot o' spent ones that'd shot their rows. They made lousy kippers because there was no real meat content on 'em.

"Before the war we used to go down to the sale-ring to buy the herrins we wanted. Us small people used to work in quite well together, but that was no use us tryin' to bid against the big firms if they'd got a large order to meet. See, they could beat you every time. Mind yuh, they were pretty good about lettin' you have some after the sales were over. Yes, you could go and ask for a cran or two and you'd usually git 'em. Do yuh know, I've bought herrins as low as half-a-crown (12½p) a cran in the 1930s! That was only occasionally, though; the normal price was about £1 or thirty bob (£1.50). I finished up payin' the equivalent o' £58 a cran when I retired in 1975. I have seen longshores make £100 a cran down on the market! That was just afore I retired, too, and they were bein' bought for the London market.

"Back before the war a lot o' the big buyers used to chuck the herrins up after they'd accepted the sample. That was done to git a re-sale and buy 'em cheaper. Yeah, they used to reckon that the herrins weren't comin' out o' the boat as good as the sample and there was hell to pay with the fishermen over that sometimes. The arbitrator would come down, or praps the salesman, and he'd git the sample and compare that with what was bein' unloaded. If he said they were all right, the buyer would have to take them. If not, they'd go up for a re-sale. The ol' Scotch curers were the boys for chuckin' up. Then you used to git the Scotch fishermen with their little fiddles. Yeah, they used to turn the baskets what they landed the herrins in upside-down and jump on 'em. That was to push the bottoms up so they wouldn't hold so many herrins! Well, some o' our blokes did that as well. Another thing was when a boat came in with a big shot and the owner used to put new baskets aboard to unload with. See, they didn't hold so much because they hadn't stretched. Well, that was the difference o' praps a stone o' fish on every basket. Hell if the buyers didn't complain!"

Curing required a lot of expertise, not only in the preparation of the fish, but in the building and controlling of the fires which effected the cure, and especially in the case of kippers. This particular method of splitting and opening the fish, then exposing it to wood-smoke, was originally practised in Scotland on salmon. It was John Woodger of Newcastle who applied the technique to herrings, producing the first kippers at Seahouses, Northumberland, in 1843. The new product caught on rapidly when it was introduced to the London market three years later.

The Raglan Street smokehouse, in which Reggie Reynolds turned out so many kippers and various other kinds of cured fish is an interesting building. The structure is of typically local brick-and-flint bond (though rendered over on three of the outside walls), with a pantile roof, and it is probably about 130 years old. Not so obviously rectangular in shape as many of Lowestoft's fish-houses, it has a double kill (or kell) incorporated within its walls – and each of these spaces measures about 12 ft in length by 8 ft width by 20 ft height. Access to both is gained through traditional stable-doors and the floors are made of brick *pamments* (the heat of the fires would crack concrete). The inside walls are encrusted with a mixture of carbon and fish-grease, and so are the loves (horizontal wooden bars fixed to the walls from just above head height to roof level) which support the rods of fish.

"I should think our Raglan Street smokehouse held about 30 to 40 cran o' herrin'. The ones we used to git durin' the Home Fishin' were about 1,000 or 1,200 to the cran. To split a herrin' for kipperin', you put your knife in the top o' the dorsal fin and you bring it down to the head. You press on your knife to go through the head and take it as far as the nose. Then you reverse your knife, stick your thumb on your free hand into the head where it's been cut, and draw the knife along the back down to the tail. The next thing is to open the herrin' out, put the knife in the gills, draw them out and draw the gut out as well. I also used to run the knife down the backbone and scrape that long streak o' blood off, because if you leave that in a kipper it looks horrible. Once the fish were split they used to be in the brine-tub anything between 15 minutes and half-an-hour, because the better the herrins the quicker they would take the salt. As regards smokin' time, I could git a kipper out in about two hours, but it wouldn't keep. Lovely for tea or breakfast next mornin', but not to travel anywhere. If I wanted 'em to keep, I'd smoke 'em overnight – anything up to about 16 hours, dependin' on the weather, because the damper it is the longer you have to keep the fires in.

"Kippers were always hung up on baulks. That was a length o' wood with cup-hook things spaced along it and each fish would be pricked on to two o' the hooks. To make the fires you used to put little heaps or lines o' wood shavings down on the floor and then cover them wi' sawdust. That was nearly all oak, o' course. We used to go and git it from Jewson's woodyard. We'd git two wheelbarrers and go down there and come back with about 15 bags o' shavings on each. There'd be some white stuff (pine) as well, because you'd need that to git the oak started. See, you only wanted the smoke; there must only be a little flame, otherwise you'd burn the bottoms o' the lowest ones above the floor. We used to git oak shavings and sawdust from local builders and undertakers as well, because oak was what gave the kippers their flavour. Some people used to use a drop o' paraffin to git the fires goin', but I never did that because it would taint the fish. I never put water on the fires either, to slow 'em down, because if you did that you'd create steam. Your kippers would go soft then and maybe fall orf the hooks. I did all my dampin' down with sawdust. You had to watch that the fires didn't burn too fierce because, as well as burnin' the bottom lot o' kippers, all the grease up the side o' the walls might catch alight.

"When you kippered Shields herrin', the floor o' the smokehouse would be that peppered with oil that if you went in with rubber boots on you'd soon be flat on your back! You used to pull the fires all over the floor when you'd finished smokin' just to soak up the grease. The oil would float to the top o' the pickle barrel and we used to skim that orf with the salt plate and put it in a bottle. That used to do to oil your boots with. Full herrins made the best kippers because they had plenty o' meat on 'em, where the *spents* were a lot thinner and drier. We never dyed our kippers either. No, my father didn't believe in that, and nor did I. There was a feller called one day and asked us to try a packet o' this vegetable dye, so we mixed it up in a big old galvanised stable-bucket and left it. We never had no intention o' usin' it. Do yuh know, that ate the bottom out o' that bucket in the end! I said to my father, 'Well, if that'll do that to a bucket, what the hell is it goin' to do to your guts?' No, we got all our colour from the natural smoke. I mean, a friend o' mine was up in Mallaig one year and he went into one o' the big fish-houses. He said it was like walkin' into a slaughterhouse. There was this red dye all over the floor and the ol' women what were workin' in the place were covered in it as well."

The practice of smoking fish seems to have been well-established by the 14th century. The herrings were either spread loose on the ground or put into troughs, then sprinkled with salt and left for varying periods of time (from a few hours to two or three days, depending on fish-quality and the desired end-product). After this they were washed and hung in the smokehouse, where they were left to cure. Again, the time varied, with the 'silver' herrings having perhaps three or four days and the 'goldens' a week or more. The fish were smoked with the gut left in. At a later date a longer, harder cure was discovered which produced the *red herring*. This product was well-known by the late 16th century when a well known Elizabethan writer celebrated its existence in a pamphlet.

Thomas Nashe, in *Lenten Stuff* (1599), claimed a number of things on behalf of the red herring. He talked of its effectiveness in combating rheumatism and gall-stones, of how it would put hounds off a scent (hence the cliché we all know) and of how, if rubbed around the rim of the vessel being used, it would remove the head on beer. The pamphlet was written largely in honour of Great Yarmouth, whither Nashe had fled from London in 1597 in order to escape the legal consequences of some satirical work he had published, but he had been born at Lowestoft of which his father was at one time Vicar. During the later decades of the 18th century the Lowestoft red herring was generally reckoned to be supreme, because the position of the smokehouses along the foot of the cliff was said to allow "an unobstructed current of air" for draughtage and ventilation.

"When you did red herrins, you wanted a good firm herrin' with a certain amount of fat in it. You could red Scotch herrins, but they weren't anything like the good local ones.

Nor were the longshores; they were very dry. Once you got to know the skippers, they'd tell you which were the herrins to buy for reds. You'd praps pay a bob or two more per cran for 'em than you would for the ordinary ones, but it was worth it. The way I used to do mine was salt 'em down on a clean concrete floor in the preparation room, next to the smokehouse. You'd spread 'em out, salt 'em well, then shovel 'em into a corner with a wooden rousin' shovel and leave 'em overnight. Next afternoon you'd give 'em some more salt and *rouse* 'em into another corner, and you'd repeat that the followin' day and praps the day after. That way they'd really take the salt. Then you used to wash 'em and speet 'em up through the mouth and the gill, with a certain number to each speet. You'd start right at the top o' your smokehouse and work down, hangin' 'em on the loves, and once you'd filled your house you put your fires down.

"You smoked reds for a couple o' months or more, but not continuously. No, you'd fire 'em one day and leave 'em the next day to sweat – otherwise you'd finish up with a very dry herrin'. If you thought they were comin' on too fast, you'd leave 'em a couple o' days without firin'. You could do what you wanted. See, you could make your fires to last an hour, two hours, three hours, or you could put fires down to last practically all day. You'd heap plenty o' dust on so they'd just smoulder. And if you could git a piece of an old apple tree and lay that on top, oh, that'd give the fish a lovely flavour! One ol' boy in the Roman Hill area used to put dried horse-muck on his fires and the reds he did were bloody beautiful! Do yuh know, I put some reds away in my mother's wash-house when I was called up in 1939 and they were still there when I got demobbed in 1945! Yeah, and I ate 'em as well. Oh yeah, they'd keep for years. And, o' course, a lot o' the pubs in the old days used to have reds for the customers to toast over the fire in the bar. They'd stand there with toastin' forks or a piece o' wire and cook these reds. That used to give 'em a real thirst. A dozen pints then, and no messin' about!

"We never did any golden or silver herrins. No. They were put in a vat before they were smoked – you know, a big hole in the ground concreted out. A firm called A.J.K., at the back of our place, used to do a lot o' them and they sent 'em to places like Greece and Italy. The fish were smoked with practically all billet wood – just a few turnings underneath to git the fires a-goin'. The smokin' time would be praps a week or a fortnight. Yeah, and the silver herrins were like bloaters and the goldens like reds – to look at, you know – and both of 'em were as salty as hell. Some o' the vats the big firms had would hold up to a hundred cran o' herrin', so that will tell yuh the size of 'em. We had a few at the back o' our place in Stanley Street, but they only held about 20 cran each.

"We used to mix up the pickle in the vat. There'd be the water go in first, then the quantity o' salt required was shot in afterwards. You'd have to git down in the vat with thigh boots on and stir it all round with a rousin' shovel till the salt was all dissolved. You tested the pickle by tasting it – you know, gittin' a handful to see if the strength was right – and you'd mix up three or four barrels to top up with. The fish used to be roused two or three times over the floor till you got to the vat, then you'd shovel 'em in and spread 'em over the vat evenly. After you'd done, you'd put boards over the vat and leave 'em. They could be in there a twelve-month. Before the war we had a Dutchman come over and buy ours. He'd take the tops off the vats, put his hand in and taste the pickle; then he'd pull out a herrin' and bite into the back – 'Yes, very good. I'll take the lot.' He used to bring his own barrels over with him, and coopers, and the herrins used to be loaded aboard a little ol' Dutch lugger and taken across to the other side. There'd be other people's aboard as well as ours. He used to go round all the small places after vatted herrins."

Kippers, reds, silvers, goldens, vatted – the only form of smoked herring not so far mentioned is the bloater. This delicacy was first devised in Great Yarmouth where it was accidentally discovered in the 1830s. A curer by the name of Bishop had some spare herrings left over at the end of a working day. Rather than dispose of them he roused them down and hung them overnight in his smokehouse. The result met with great approval and from then on herrings were cured in that particular way as a commercial proposition. Heat was rather more important in the process than smoke and the end-product could often be of superlative flavour, though best if eaten within a day of curing.

"I never gave my bloaters less than four hours in the salt and I used to speet 'em straight out o' the brine so they were semi-washed. They were stuck through the mouth and the gill, like a red and I used to hang 'em on the rack after that and just give 'em a fine sprinkle o' water to clean any muck orf before I hung 'em in the smokehouse. There was no guttin' or anything with 'em, so there wasn't a lot o' messin' around. You can git a bloater out in about a couple o' hours smokin', but they'd soon go damp and they wouldn't keep. I used to smoke mine overnight. I'd build three or four fires just before I finished work and then I'd go in first thing in the mornin' and see how they were. I used to feel 'em all the way along the bottoms because that was where they got done first. I smoked sprats as well. Yeah, we had special little speets for them. They'd be in the pickle about half to three-quarters of an hour, then in the smokehouse for about four or five hours. A lot o' the people did wind-dried herrins in their own backyards. Yeah, they'd have 'em strung up on a line near the back door. All they used to do was rub the herrins down in some rough salt and then hang 'em out to dry.

"My hands used to be cracked to blazes with the salt. Yeah, I was forever rubbin' 'em with vaseline and goin' to bed with gloves on! The only trouble was that once they cracked open, they'd stay open because you were always dippin' your hands into brine. The poor ol' Scotch girls were just the same when they were *gyppin'* herrins on the picklin' plots. All the salt we used came down from Cheshire on the railway. Mitchell and Hobson were two o' the big agents for that. They had salt stores on the north side o' the quay, up-through bridge near the dry-dock, and you used to go down there for whatever you wanted.

"Herrins were our main thing, o' course, but we also did a certain amount o' trawl fish. We used to cure 'em in the red herrin' side o' the fish-house when the reds weren't in there. See, we only did reds Home Fishin' time and over Christmas, so that left the kill spare the rest o' the time. Haddicks was what we done mostly, but there'd be whitings and cod as well. I've smoked place, soles, ling, gurnets, latchets, catfish and monks. They're all lovely as long as they're done right. I usually gave 'em about ten minutes in the brine and would then smoke 'em anything between six and twelve hours. That all depended on what you wanted. My father used to do bacon and hams for some o' the grocery shops in town and I remember he had a side o' pork there once that was alive wi' maggots. You could see the skin all movin' and as soon as he put his knife into it and slit along, there they all were! I suppose the funniest thing I ever smoked was a pike what some bloke brought in. He'd caught it in Oulton Broad, and when I opened it up I found a damn great rat inside! Yeah, I've never seen anything like that, before or since."

A load of barrels ready for use on a Yarmouth pickling plot around 1910. The barrels have iron end hoops, with the intermediary bands made of split ash wood.

CHAPTER SEVEN

Factory Processes

'Let Lent well kept offend not thee,
For March and Aprill breeders bee:
Spend herring first, save saltfish last,
For saltfish is good when Lent is past.'
('Five Hundred Points Of Good Husbandry' – Thomas Tusser)

The massed lines of tins on supermarket shelves containing food of one kind or another have their origins in military requirements. It was in 1809 that Nicholas Appert perfected the method of preserving perishable foodstuffs by heat processing, with the object of provisioning Napoleon's army and navy. Appert used glass jars, but an Englishman called Peter Durand soon invented and patented steel cans, and by the late 1830s tin-coated steel containers were being produced on a large scale.

During the 1870's two Lowestoft fish merchants, James and Archibald Maconochie, were running a food factory in Raglan Street and such was its success that in the 1890's they were able to build a smart new premises on part of the old Kirkley parish waste lands. They chose as their spot the western side of an inlet off Lowestoft's inner harbour, known as Kirkley Ham, on the other side of which was the notable shipyard founded in 1876 by the Cornishman, Sam Richards. The whole of the former Maconochie complex has been owned since the 1920's by the Cooperative Wholesale Society and, with all the additions and refinements made over the intervening years, it is now said to be the largest canning factory in Western Europe. Stella Walpole (born 1900) worked in the Maconochie factory during and after the First World War.

"I worked at a dairy when I left school, doin' a milk round with a pony and cart. Then I went to Maconochie's factory when I was about 15 or 16. There was about two or three of us from Corton – you know, girls from the village – and we used to bike in. We were always gittin' punctures, so we used to ride with flat tyres. Yeah, and sometimes we used to git the front wheel stuck in the tramlines goin' down the High Street and then we'd go sprawlin'. I've been spilt in the street like that more'n once. But, there you are, you had to git across the bridge and git to work on time. O' course, we often used to catch a bridger. Yeah, that'd be open to let ships through by the time we got there. So what we used to do then was git one o' the men in the bridge-house to phone the factory and tell 'em we were held up. There was one man there on the gate, who'd come out o' the army early because he'd got a war wound, and he used to lock us out. He'd wait for us to come scorchin' down the hill after a bridger, then he'd lock us out on purpose. Cor, them girls dint half swear at him. 'Serve yuh right,' he used to say. 'You should git here on time.'

"Durin' the war we were doin' rations for the troops. Yeah, tins o' beef and vegetables and little oval cans o' drippin'. They were all sent abroad, out to the front. We worked on piecework and I reckon we were earnin' up to about £3 a week, which was a lot o' money in them days. When we were workin' overtime, we used to nip down to the Belvedere pub to git a drink and that used to be lovely. O' course, we didn't always want to do the overtime, but we had to. Yes, the foreman used to come round and say, 'I want you, an' you, an' you.' One day I bopped down behind the machine so he didn't notice me. 'I can see yuh boppin' down,' he say. 'You can git up. You're workin' tonight.' We used to work all the week and a half-day on Saturday, and we'd be goin' sometimes from six o' clock in the mornin' till ten at night. That was dangerous, too, with them machines. One o' the girls got dragged in by the arm and that'd nearly been pulled orf by the time the engineer heard her shoutin' and came and turned the machine off. They took her to hospital and she had to lose the arm. We got bombed there once as well. I can remember that all right! Oh, that was dreadful!"

"After the war we did canned fish – you know, fresh herrins, kippers, roes an' fish paste. There was a quay at the factory and the boats used to come right up there and land. Oh yeah, the Hoom Fishin' was a right busy time. We had Scotch gals on the quay, guttin' the fish, and then some o' us used to cart 'em up into the factory to be tinned. The smokehouses for doin' the kippers used to be in Raglan Street, I think. Yeah, I don't remember any smokehouses at the factory. Them roes we did used to be beautiful. We used to do 'em separate, the hard ones and the soft. All the stuff in the cans had to be cooked in steam ovens, o' course, an' then properly sealed afterwards. The cans used to be lacquered as well, to make 'em look nice and shiny, an' then there was a special room where girls used to put the labels on.

"After the war we went orf piecework an' got paid by the hour. They used to reckon it up in quarters, and they'd soon cut yuh orf a quarter of an hour's pay if you were late! When we got paid at the end o' the week, we had to go along to the office, take our numbers orf a big board they had on the wall outside, call 'em out and git the money. The wages used to be paid out in little tins. Yeah, everybody had one, and after you'd took your money out you used to chuck the tin into a box they had stand there because they wanted the tins back to use next week. We didn't work the hours that we had done on the rations. Oh no, they wouldn't let us put in that sort o' time. But we did do overtime on the Hoom Fishin'.

"They had a Scotch manager there at Maconochie's. Well, they had three or four altogether, but one was in complete charge. A couple of 'em used to live in them two big houses opposite the factory, so they were right on the spot. There was one or two women as well (Buckie, we used to call one of 'em) and they'd make yuh work just as hard as the men. Yeah, there was no playin' about wi' them ol' Scotch people. The stuff used to go away from the factory on horses an' carts an' lorries; that used to be took up to the railway station, I expect. Across the road, over opposite the factory, there was a bit o' waste ground where they used to bury all the cans what didn't seal properly. *Dennies*, they called 'em. Yeah, they used to open 'em out, throw away what was in 'em and then go bury 'em. I reckon if people were to dig down there now, they'd find some Maconochie tins, even though there's houses on parta o' the land. O' course, another thing we used to make, which was nothin' to do with the fish stuff, was raspberry and strawberry jam. Oh yeah, and fondant sweets as well. When that was our dinner-hour, we sometimes used to nip into the room where they were made an' git a handful!

"We used to do herrins in tomato sauce. There'd be four or five herrins packed in a tin and then so much tomato sauce put on. The tins used to come along a belt and go through a machine which put the lids on. I was on that machine one day, a-puttin' the tins through, and there was a manager from the London factory standin' there watchin' me. Do yuh know, them girls back down the line began to send the tins down quicker so I couldn't keep up with 'em. Yeah, and some of 'em finished up on the floor, right in front o' that man from London. They were laughin' like the devil, them girls were! I wun't, though. I was swearin' to myself. In the factory the men used to do all the heavy work, and liftin' and that, and o' course they used to look after the machines as well. We used to have some laughs with the engineers. Yeah, whenever a machine broke down, they used to reckon that was our fault. We soon used to tell 'em, though. Yis, that we did.

"That was nice workin' at Maconochie's. You got all different sorts o' people and everyone got to know each other. Well, you had to, just to keep sociable, didn't yuh? A lot o' the girls used to sing as they worked and that sounded lovely. I was singin' away there one day, not lookin' what I was doin', and I got burnt by some hot jam. Me and this other girl were pushin' a bogie along, with a tub o' hot jam on it, and that sloshed out over my hands. I was singin' 'Show Me The Way To Go Home', but I soon stopped singin' when the jam splashed on me. I had to go down to the first-aid room at the office and I got told orf for messin' about. They put me on a light job till my hands got properly better. Yeah, they had me packin' tins. That was still hard on the legs, though – just like all factory work. See, you used to be standin' so long. We used to look forward to dinnertime, so we could go outside an' sit on the grass. We went in the meal-room when the weather was bad. See, they had a room there where you could eat your grub and that had cookin' stoves in it as well. Yeah, and there was women in charge o' them who'd cook anything you brought in, or warm it up for yuh, so you could have a hot meal in the middle o' the day.

"One year, when Maconochie's stood some of us orf 'cause there wun't much work about, we went and got a job at Morton's. This was after the Hoom Fishin', when things were a bit slack, but for some reason Morton's were settin' people on. They did all fish there from what I can remember and the boats used to come and land at their quay, like they did at Maconochie's. We were tinnin' herrins and kippers just the same, but I never liked it as much somehow. No, I was more used to Maconochie's, yuh see, and I didn't like the foreman they had at Morton's very much either. He was a strict ol' man and he used to git a big trolley in the middle o' the room an' stand up on that so he could see everything what you were doin'. And he used to point his finger at yuh, too. Oh, I couldn't stick that!"

Frozen fish, which we now all take so much for granted, was to come much later. Frank Bristow (born 1913) was the son of a traditional Yarmouth smoker, but went into a canning factory as a young man. He went into the army at the beginning of the Second World War. When he emerged seven years later a new revolution in the fishing industry awaited him.

"I came out o' the forces on July 1st, 1947, and I started work the next day. I'd got a job with Herring Industries Ltd through an advert my wife had seen in the *Lowestoft Journal*. It said that a manager for a herring cold-store plant was required, but that experience of cold storage was not necessary. Well, I didn't know the first thing about cold storage, but I applied for the job and got it. I started straight away because they wanted someone to prepare for the Home Fishing. Before Herring Industries took it over, the firm had been known as L. A. Robinson. The original Robinson was a farmer in the area who'd started the quick freezing of herring and he'd handed the business on to his son, Leslie. Leslie Robinson sold out to Associated Fisheries and this is where I came in. The premises mainly consisted of smoking facilities, but there was a freezing plant and a small cold store of about 20,000 cubic feet capacity. It stood on Whapload Road, opposite the Rising Sun public house. That first Home Fishing we were freezing herrings and we were also putting them down in vats for silvers and goldens. We had about ten vats altogether and each one held about 100 crans.

"Now, the powers-that-be were encouraged by the success of the herrings we froze in 1947 and they agreed that our future lay in freezing and cold-storage. So, in a matter of a few years, all the smoking and vatting facilities had been dispensed with, all the dilapidated buildings had been knocked down, and everything had gone over to cold-storage. I suppose we increased our capacity from 20,000 cubic feet to something like 200,000 and we also went through three different freezing processes. When I first started there, the method was to freeze the herrings by having them pass down spiral flumes and letting very cold brine percolate onto them. After that they went through a freshwater flume down into a pit, where a man packed them into wooden boxes to go into the store. Then, about 1950, we changed over to blast-freezing. We used ammonia to get a very low temperature and a huge fan would blow this cold air over the herrings. Oh, it was enough to take your trousers off, if you see what I mean! Finally, by about the mid 50's we started contact freezing. Ammonia was the refrigerant again, but instead of the herrings being done singly they were put on metal trays and frozen into seven pound blocks by a hydraulic compress.

"All the herrings were frozen ungutted, of course, and we had two export markets for them in Australia and Poland. Mind you, our biggest outlet was the local merchants. Yes, we provided a sheet-anchor for them at times o' the year when fresh herrings weren't available. They could draw on our supplies, thaw them out, and make kippers, bloaters and bucklings. One of our associated companies used to do bucklings. Yes, they had Jewish connections in Whitechapel and round that way and bucklings were very popular with the Jewish people. I didn't actually buy herrings down on the Lowestoft market because we had a buyer working for us there on an agency basis, but I did go out buying longshores on Sunday mornings at various local places – Corton, Kessingland, Southwold etc. Yes, I liked to do that because very few drifters would land on a Monday morning, so if I was able to buy on the Sunday there would be a good day's work for freezing on the Monday.

"Down in Ness Road another of our associated companies, the British & American Salmon Curing Co., used to do marinated herrings in barrels, which were then sent up to our place to be chilled and stored. The fish were gutted and opened out by machine, then steeped in acetic acid flavoured with bay leaves and black peppers. They used to go down to one of our London factories eventually to be turned into roll mops in 12 ounce jars. During the disastrous winter flood of 1953 about 1,000 barrels o' these marinated herrings were swept out of the Ness Road yard. It took a small army o' men and hired lorries almost the whole of the following week to recover them and, at the final count, only 20 barrels had been lost. It speaks volumes for the skill of the cooper (Alec Smith, an Aberdonian) that the condition of the fish was unaffected.

"Another of our freezing lines was sprats. Yes, we used to do enormous quantities o' them for canning firms, so that when they couldn't get fresh ones they could draw upon their frozen supplies and keep the factories going with brisling and so forth. We had one or two contracts for frozen sprats in Sweden and Poland, and in order to keep all our customers happy we used to buy the fish wherever we could. Oh yes, I'd go out buying longshores, just like I did with the herrings; and when the local season finished in about March, we used to have sprats come up by road and by rail from Poole and Torquay and Brixham. They'd be well iced, you see, in barrels or boxes, and they'd be very welcome in April and onwards for the canning people to draw on.

"Soon after I began working for Herring Industries Ltd., we started to do a little work in trawl-fish. Fish was still on allocation then, but Associated Fisheries (which was the parent company) was represented on the market and eligible for a share, so a certain amount came our way. After a while the trawl-fish side got bigger and bigger. I mean, when the sprat season came to an end, we used to freeze fillets of plaice. The local merchants used to send them in, we'd freeze them into seven pound blocks in the contact freezers, and then they'd be drawn out later. A lot of that stuff was utilised for the summer holiday trade at Yarmouth, guest-houses and hotels and fish-and-chip shops. We used to freeze turbots as well (whole ones), and brill. We did codling (loads and loads o' that), But not very much whiting. They were both filleted, o' course, and so were the haddocks. Then there were the Dover soles and lemon soles. We did a lot o' fillets o' those and they went down to London to one of our companies, which wanted them for the shipping trade. P.&O. was a big customer for various fillets o' sole. Some local merchants used to send dogfish and roker in to be frozen, but we never bought it ourselves. No, we were never very keen because there's a certain ammonia content in them and it might quickly become apparent once the fish came into contact with the cold. There was no problem with shellfish, though, and we used to store a certain quantity o' shrimps and prawns for local people.

"Whatever we handled and held on behalf of the various merchants we charged for. They had to pay a freezing charge and then a rental for the time their fish was in the store. When the main trawl fishing season came to an end and all the local stuff was stock-piled, we used to freeze fish for the biggest firm of all, just up the road – Birds Eye. That would be during the summer, when they couldn't handle a lot o' fish because they were busy with the peas. Sometimes we froze peas for them at peak times and we used to do soft fruits as well – plus considerable quantities o' strawberry puree, which used to finish up in Walls ice-cream. Then there was the oven ready poultry we did, turkeys and chickens. That was a good line. Yes, and one of the people we used to freeze for at one time was Bernard Matthews. I suppose that was before he'd got his own facilities.

"Associated Fisheries closed the Lowestoft cold-store in 1969 for economic reasons. We'd had some wonderfully lucrative years, but we'd suddenly come to a crossroads. The herring fishing had died out, Salvesen's had built their huge cold-store complex over at Oulton Broad, and Birds Eye had expanded their capacity. Associated Fisheries therefore decided that it was no longer a viable economic proposition to remain in Lowestoft."

Another phase of the fishing industry's changing fortunes had been reached and Frank Bristow took an early retirement.

Employees of Morton's canning factory in Lowestoft on a works outing by charabanc in the 1920's. (Courtesy Jack Rose)

CHAPTER EIGHT

Boxes And Tins

'Light she was like a fairy,
And her shoes were number nine;
Herring boxes without topses
Sandals were for Clementine.'
('Clementine' – Percy Montrose)

Large quantities of timber were once brought into Lowestoft to make all kinds of boxes and containers for herrings and trawl-fish. Sailing vessels from Scandanavia and the Baltic ports used to be a regular sight in the town and their latter-day, diesel-engined successors continue to pass in and out of the harbour, though their cargoes of pine and spruce are intended for the custom-built joinery trade. Jewson & Sons Ltd., the firm referred to as a source of *shruff* for curing in chapter six is still in existence, though its mainstream activities have for several years now been connected with the building trade. It still occupies the same site in Belvedere Road, a thoroughfare whose name derives from Belvedere Works in Lambeth, part of the business empire of Samuel Morton Peto, the great Victorian contractor who developed Lowestoft in the 1840's. Jewson's also had a yard on the south side of the harbour where Arthur Collins (born 1914) worked in the box-making trade.

"My father was the skipper o' the *Queen of Devon* (LT83), a smack. She was blown up by a mine on December 20th, 1914, and all the crew were lost. My oldest brother was deckhand on her and he went down too. That happened a week before I was born and I was entered on the roll o' dependents in the Low'stoft Fisherman's Widows and Orphans Fund the day that I was born. My mother said I was the youngest one they'd ever had on their books. When I was a boy, I used to go with her to an office about three-quarters o' the way down Commercial Road to draw the allowance. That was about half-a-crown (12½p) a week, I think. After the war my mother got married again to a man who'd been a stoker in the Navy. He was a very hardworking man, my stepfather. Yes, he'd do anything in order to keep in a job. When I was very little, we lived in Mariners Street and my mother farmed me out to Mariners Score school when I was only three so she could go out to work to keep the fam'ly. Later on we moved down onto The Beach, into Wilde's Street, and then when I was about 17 we all shifted up to Pakefield.

"When we lived on The Beach, us kids used to go down on the fish market and pick up herrins orf the lower landin'. They used to fall out o' the baskets as the crew were unloadin' the boat, and a meal was a meal in them days! Sometimes Mother would send us down to ol' Tommy Jones's fish-house at the end o' Wilde's Street to git three penn'orth (1½p) o' second-grade kippers. There was nothin' wrong with 'em to eat. They were wonderful kippers, all oak-smoked, but praps the head had got a bit torn where it had been pulled orf the hook. I attended Wilde's School, o' course, and I left at Christmas 1928, when I was in standard six. That was one o' the free schools in Low'stoft originally and there was a big motto on the gable end o' the classroom wall: 'Bring up a child in the way it should go and it will never depart from it.' Mother wouldn't let me go out on the boats, yuh know. No, she'd had enough o' the sea. I mean, it wasn't just my father and oldest brother who got lost. My next eldest brother was cook on the smack *Chrysolite* (LT 635) when she got blown up in 1917."

German U-boats exacted a heavy toll among the Lowestoft fleet of sailing trawlers during the First World War, but there was also loss of life during peace-time. The risk factor in fishing received official recognition in 1877, when the January gale of that year resulted in seven smacks going to the bottom with all hands. The financial appeal launched by local dignitaries on this occasion was made a permanent foundation in the establishment of the Lowestoft Fishermen's Widows And Orphans Fund. The trust is still in existence and continues to aid the dependents of fishermen lost at sea. Young Arthur Collins was one of many beneficiaries over the years and his education, too, was partly the result of even earlier public-spirited action. In 1735 John Wilde, merchant, endowed a free school for 40 boys in his last will and testament. He also left, among other things, one guinea per year to the Vicar of Lowestoft, on condition that an annual sermon was preached every December 23rd in St. Margaret's parish church on the text, 'Train up a child'. It was this quotation from Proverbs 22 that decorated the wall of the classroom.

"My mother happened to know the under-foreman at Jewson's and that's how I came to go there in the January o' 1929. I started orf making red herrin ' boxes for Morton's and I was using inch nails. I had to pack the boxes into a great big laundry-basket thing on wheels and trundle 'em across the road to the factory. O' course, they were making all sorts o' things there in the yard – horseshoe boxes for the Army, shell cases for the Army and the Navy, and bomb boxes for the Air Force. Oh, we did a lot o' work for the Gover'ment over the years, and it was all done by hand and screwdrivers – no machinery at all. The handles used to be made o' rope and they were all hand riveted onto the boxes. The firm used to employ old fishermen to make the handles and do all the splicin'. Even when we got case-making machinery in the works, the gover'ment stuff continued to be made by hand. Do yuh know, we used to make cases half as big as this room we're sitting in for parts o' aeroplanes to go in!

"Another big thing used to be the boxes for the local fish merchants in the town, people like Podd, Cladingbowl, Mummery and Easto. We did a lot o' what was called margarines. They were a smallish box and they were all done by hand, until we got the machines in. Mind you, the machines only made the box itself; the metal bands put round had to be done by hand. We made no end o' klondyke cases durin' the summer as well. Yes, they used to be got ready for the Home Fishin'. They were quite a large case, a bit too big really to make on a machine, so what we used to do was make the ends on a machine and then assemble 'em by hand. They were put together with two-inch nails and we made thousands of 'em. Well, you used to see great big stacks o' them standin' in various places all over town. Oh, there was a lot o' money in klondykin'. Another thing we used to do was make kipper boxes for a Hull firm called Andrew Johnson & Knudtzon (A.J.K.) That was the father o' Amy Johnson and we did a lot o' boxes for him. He had his own distinctive stencil made, which was always printed in red.

"We made a non-returnable fish box for some o' the trawl firms. W. H. Podd had a lot o' them. The way it came about was that we got a wood-slicin' machine, which was very fast and could slice the wood both down the length and across the grain. It was a great big wheel with two blades set in it, and it used to go through a piece o' wood like a railway sleeper as quick as anything. The finish was good too, so we used to make thousands o' chocolate boxes on that for Caley's factory in Norwich. Other things we were doin' in the yard included tomato boxes and all kinds o' trays and then there were the special things like the brewery boxes. They were quite a substantial thing because they were made to hold bottles, and we did them for nearly all the local concerns: Bullards; Steward & Patterson; Adnams o' Southwold; Lacons o' Yarmouth; Youngs, Crawshay & Youngs; Morgans; Tolly Cobbold. Do yuh know, there was even a time (getting towards 1939) when we were making parts of accomodation quarters for troops! Yeah, the gable-end section o' huts. We made thousands upon thousands o' those.

"Our timber came from Russia mostly – Archangel and round that area – and I think we got some from Finland as well. It was all white wood, though we did use hardwood ends on the gover'ment boxes. Oh yes, it was all the best timber for gover'ment stuff. The ships used to come right up opposite the works and sometimes they would discharge part o' their cargo over at our place in Yarmouth. I think that the labourers who unloaded the timber ships got 10½d (5p) an hour and the ones in the yard were on the same amount. Us boxmakers were on piecework, though. Yes, we used to start at half-past seven in the mornin' and finish at half-past five – except on Saturdays, when we knocked orf at 12 o' clock. There were no holidays then, except the annual ones like Christmas Day and Boxing Day, and we used to have to work hard to earn our money. We made sure we earnt it too, though I can't remember now what the rates were. I know the firm tried to get us to go on an hourly rate at one time, but we preferred to stay on piece-work. We worked as a body o' people, all doin' the different kinds o' boxes, and the foreman had the jurisdiction of all the money. He allocated that at the end o' the week. I can't remember now what I earned when I became experienced, but I know that I started in the yard at ten shillins (50p) a week. I was known as 'the boy' then – you're always 'the boy' when you start work, aren't yuh! – but as I got older and more proficient, my money went up.

"We used to put in plenty o' overtime there on occasions on the box-makin'. Yes, if you got a lot o' orders come in, you'd work from praps six in the mornin' till half-past seven at night to get 'em out. There was no playin' about then! Oh no! You kept your nose down to the job. The foreman used to accept the price from the bosses for all the different kinds o' work (there was a rate for each class, you see) and then he'd pay you out yuh wages at the end o' the week. Priority used to be given to the local fish merchants, because when they wanted boxes they wanted 'em there and then. Tomorrow or the next day was no good; they wanted 'em down on the market there and then near enough. Oh, we used to keep very busy, though there were one or two slack times when we got laid orf. The box-trade was quite an important part o' local industry. Latten's were doin' the same thing, and then you got other firms like Wenn's o' Yarmouth. Jewson's had their own horses and carts in my early days there and they were followed later on by lorries. There was a railway siding right alongside the yard as well and these great big shire horses used to pull the trucks down and take 'em away loaded up with all different boxes and cases. Later on the railway people went in for those three-wheeled tractor things, but horses were very much the vogue before that."

Arthur Collins had joined the Territorial Army in 1937, so with the outbreak of hostilities in 1939 quickly found himself a full time soldier. After the war he went to work in the canning factory of C. E. Morton Ltd., a firm that had come down to Lowestoft from Aberdeen in 1901 specifically to cure and can herrings.

"Morton's were advertisin' for a storekeeper at the time and it was only just over the road, so I thought that I'd apply for it. I didn't get it, but the next week I got a letter asking if I would be interested in a job as under-supervisor in their pickle-room department. Well, I went and had an interview and got offered the job. The only thing was it was worth less than I was getting at Jewson's. I took it, though, because Morton's had just been taken over by the Beecham group, and I thought that with a big firm like that there must be prospects. The manager gave me six weeks to learn the job and I soon managed to pick it up – how to fortify the vinegar and all that sort o' thing. We were doing mixed pickles in ten ounce jars and we did up to 10,000 o' them in a day. Yes, we had rows o' girls packin' cauliflower, gherkins and silverskin onions in the jars. We had our own pickle boats come over from Holland with cauliflowers and cucumbers and onions, and they used to land on our own quay. Oh, that was quite a big thing in its day, but in the end it died a natural death.

"As soon as the Home Fishing started, everything went over to herrins. The drifters used to come up-through-bridge and land on our quay and we also had lorries bring stuff up from the fish market. Charlie Osborne was our buyer down there. We used to make our own kits, by the way. Oh yes, we had coopers on the staff. When the herrins arrived at the factory, they would go to the knobbing machines which cut off the heads and squeezed the guts out. Then they were put into vats, washed around in brine, left in for so long, and eventually taken out and sent to the packing lines. There they were weighed into either 14 ounce or seven ounce lots and put into tins, either as fresh herrins in brine or as herrins in tomato sauce. The tins were flat, oval ones and the Morton's people liked to get three herrins in the big tins and two in the small ones. Sometimes you had to cut a piece orf the top o' the herrins to get two in a seven ounce tin. After the fish were packed, the tins used to go through an exhauster to get the air out and a seamer to seal the lid on. Then they went into the retorts to be cooked.

"We did rows as well. They were packed into seven ounce tins, either as hard or soft, and we had quite a good trade in them. See, we used to tin kippers for export, Australia and New Zealand and places, and we had splitting machines to get the herrins ready for curin'. There was quite a number o' smokehouses there at the factory and then, in the end, the management got a smokin' machine to speed the job up. That was like a great big oven and it cut down the time needed for the smokin' side. Back before the war Morton's used to do a lot o' red herrins and they had their own underground pits where they used to store the fish before they were cured. They'd finished with 'em by the time I went there, but the herrin' season was still a big thing. Oh yes, we had six or seven lines battin' out the tins. Sometimes we used to get in extra supplies down from Scotland, but the Home Fishing was the main season. When that died away, o' course, canning herrins died away with it, so the firm had to go into other things. We used to do a fish paste, which was mostly made out o' whiting, and then there were all the other various products. O' course, the factory was originally built for herrins, just like Maconochie's. There was a lot o' herrins done at that place as well when it became the Co-op."

The decline of the North Sea herring stocks made a considerable difference to Morton's factory, as it terminated a number of successful and long-established lines. The last fish products were canned in 1956.

Arthur and his colleagues had to adapt themselves to the processing of peas, fruit and pie fillings to keep the factory viable.

"It's just how things change. I mean, when I was a boy, everything in this town was connected with fishing. It was all fish-boxes at Jewson's; a lot o' the girls were put to work as beatsters; there were Scotch curin' yards all over the place; and the klondykin' was goin' full bang. People used to work all night to load up the klondyke boats and the roads used to get in a terrible state with all the maise an' stuff comin' out o' the herrins. Nobody minded, though. It was a living."

CHAPTER NINE

The Ice Factory

'Now when we git our fish on board we have them all to gut.
We hull them all in baskets and down the ice-locker put.
We ice them down, we size them, we ice them all quite well.
We ice them an' keep them safely as an oyster in his shell.'
('The Smacksman' – traditional)

The introduction of ice to preserve catches of fish is attributed to Samuel Hewett of Barking, in the 1840s. He did it to keep his trawling smacks at sea for lengthy periods (four to six weeks) when they were working the Dogger Bank during the winter months. Before that fish was kept alive in water-filled holds or 'wells' and taken into port after ten days or so for unloading. When boats began to ice the catches on board they transferred them at sea to fast sailing cutters which ran the fish down to Billingsgate, enabling the smacks to keep trawling. This so-called 'fleeting' method of fishing was much more profitable though notoriously hard on the crews, and the use of ice increased considerably in the second half of the century.

Samuel Hewett's early supplies were collected by local farmers from the ditches of the Essex marshes, with the season usually beginning in mid November. Most of this ice was thin and it commanded a price of two shillings (10p) a ton when plentiful and four shillings (20p) when scarce. As the weather got colder, the thicker ice which formed was sawn out of the ditches and sold at five shillings (25p) a ton. As demand increased supplies were imported from the Norwegian fjords.

Norwegian ice was also used in Lowestoft as the trawling industry developed during the 1860s and 70s, but local supplies were used whenever a cold spell produced it. Wherries brought cargoes in from the Norfolk and Suffolk Broads and the marshes around. But the 1890's demand had led to the formation of ice-importing companies in the port.

There were two main concerns and one of them, the Lowestoft Ice Company, sold 1,440 tons of Norwegian ice in 1875. By 1882 sales had risen to 6,000 tons, with the price going up from 21 shillings (£1.05) to 35 shillings (£1.75) a ton over the same period. In 1898 the East Anglian Ice Company was set up to manufacture this precious commodity without being dependent on the weather. From an initial output of something like 10,000 to 12,000 tons a year, it increased its capacity to around 40,000 tons by the late 1950s, with a new factory opening in 1962. Arthur Pitcher (born 1905) was employed at both places.

"I started in 1922 and went in the engine-room, greasin'. We worked a shift system – six o' clock till two, two till ten and ten till six – and there were three men on each shift, with another three on reliefs. There was a stoker, who kept the boilers goin'; a driver, who looked after the engines and the refrigeration side; and a greaser, who greased up and oiled round. We had three water-tube boilers there, a big Robey steam engine and two smaller ones. The Robey used to make about 150 tons o' ice a day and the other two about 25 ton each. Most o' the machinery was all open and you had to catch the cross-head with an oil-feeder when it was in motion just to make sure you kept it oiled. All the bearings had bottles on and you had to keep them filled up with oil or things would start to heat up. After you'd been greasin' for a certain length o' time, you got made up to driver when the opportunity came and then you found yourself in charge o' all the engines. That big Robey we had there was a one-cylinder job of about 900 horse-power. It revved at about 150 to the minute and it had a flywheel which weighed 12 ton! We used it to belt drive most o' the machinery in the factory, like the agitators and things, and it also worked the big compressor for makin' the ice.

"They still work on the same principles down at the new factory, more or less. See, you use ammonia to do the freezin'. You have that circulatin' all the time, both as liquid and gas. It only freezes as a gas, so you have to force the liquid through the expansion valve. You pump it into the valve at a pressure of about 150/160 pounds per square inch (in hot weather it used to go up to 170) and it turns into gas. The gas is then drawn through coils submerged in brine, which is where you make your ice, and after that it goes back into the machine to be compressed into a liquid again. By the time it's been through the brine tanks it's gettin' pretty hot so you have to cool it down and condense it back. We had a series o' coils on the outside o' the machine down at the old factory and we used to pump water out o' the river to do the coolin' down. The whole process is a continuous circulation, yuh see – expand into a gas, freeze, warm up, condense into a liquid, and round again.

"The brine we used for freezin' was made from calcium chloride and each tank o' brine we had held 28 rows o' cans o' fresh water. We used the town water, orf the mains, and there were 24 cans to each row. The brine used to circulate around the cans (it was kept on the move with agitators) and each o' the cans held two hundredweight o' ice. The temperature o' the brine was about 16°F in the early mornin' in the summer and that would go up to about 24°F or 25°F as the day went on. If you were making a lot o' ice, that raised the temperature of the brine as well, but it never went above 26°F. The water in the cans were tap temperature, o' course, and you had to lose that heat before freezin' started. The whole process used to take up to about 48 hours to get a good, solid block o' ice, although sometimes when we were a bit rushed we used to get the blocks out before they were fully made up. A crane used to lift the cans up out o' the brine tank, submerge 'em into a big tank o' warm water (that was heated by steam coils) to loosen the blocks, and then drop 'em down into a turntable. The blocks used to shoot out then down onta the ice-floor and the crane would return the empty cans to be refilled with fresh water and put back into the brine tank. All the rows o' cans were pushed through the tank very slowly by buffer gear until freezin' was complete. Then the crane would come along, lift the end row out, empty the cans and return 'em to the far end o' the tank. It was all a continuous process. We had two big tanks with 28 rows o' cans in at 24 to the row and a smaller one with 16 to the row.

"Once the blocks o' ice were on the ice-floor, the blokes there would git hold of 'em with ice-tongs and put 'em into the crusher. That was a big drum with iron spikes on, driven by belt orf the big Robey engine, and it used to crush the blocks up as it went round. Then the ice used to go up a bucket elevator into a big hopper and you used to load up the horses and carts out o' that. There were two spouts on it and you could block one orf as the other was bein' used. The horses and carts and lorries used to pull up underneath that with a load o' kits and fill up. Cor, when the klondykin' was on, I've seen horses and carts stretchin' from our quay right up Horn Hill and out o' sight, waitin' to take on ice.

"Our factory was at the bottom o' Riverside Road, down past the Co-op, and we had our own bit o' quay there. That's where our ice-wherries used to load up to go down to the market. We had four o' them, all motor-driven, and they used to hold about 28 to 30 ton each. The ice used to go out over the edge o' the quay through a worm gear down into the wherries and that was trimmed into the hold so's to be all level. Then the hatches were fitted tight over the top and a tarpaulin put over to keep the air out. The wherries used to carry baskets on board and they were used to put the ice aboard o' the trawlers. Some o' the trawlers used to come up to our quay. Yeah, they'd say, 'We want ten ton o' ice.' What we used to do was put the spout down into the hold, count the right number o' blocks into the crusher, and when that'd all gone through that was his lot. The drifters never came up to the quay because they didn't take much ice on board. They only took about half a ton or a ton, so they got what they wanted orf the wherries. See, the only time they used ice was when there weren't many herrins about. Normally, they liked to git a catch and come in and land. When things were short, they'd ice the herrins down and keep out another night to try and git some more. Then, if they got a catch, they'd come in. And, o' course, the iced herrins they had didn't make as much money as the freshuns did.

"Our really busy time was durin' the Home Fishing', especially when the klondykin' really got started. Yeah, in the summer you'd make about 150 ton a day, but that'd go up to over 200 ton in the herrin' season. What we used to do was fill the ice-floor right up at weekends, so we had about 200 ton to start with on the Monday. We had a storeroom, too, which held about 600 ton and we used that to draw on as well. It was the old original place, with a wooden inner wall and the cavity space filled with sawdust and stuff, and we used to pump the brine round that to keep the temperature down.

"Most o' the ice we made was opaque and we used to charge the drifters and trawlers about 18 shillins (90p) a ton for it. Same with the exporters; that'd be about the price they paid. But we used to have a lot o' other customers as well, yuh know, like fishmongers and butchers and milkmen. Oh yeah, they all used to come down and we charged them about a shillin' (5p) a hundredweight. A lot of 'em used to come down with wheelbarrers in the old days and all they'd want was about six penn'orth (2½p) o' ice. You used to git a lot o' little icecream merchants as well, and some o' them used to come down with a sack to git their six penn'orth in. Oh, we got everybody! When I first went down there, we were makin' clear ice in a big three ton block. It was much more expensive than the opaque because it took a week to make. All the water had to be properly agitated to take the air bubbles out and you used to finish up with a nice clear ice. Most o' that used to go up to Norwich on an ol' sailing wherry, skippered by a man called Billy Royall, and that was used in the various butchers' and fishmongers' shops. They used to have a lump of it in their windows with stuff on top, but once fridges started to come in there was no demand for it. After a while we converted the clear ice tank into makin' the opaque. Yeah, we put hundreweight cans in it so they could go through in half the time – 24 hours instead o' 48.

"At one time o' day people used to cut ice out o' Oulton Broad durin' the winter. And then, when they couldn't git that, they used to bring it in from the fjords o' Norway. Yeah, when I first went to the Ice Company, if we couldn't make enough, that would be brought in from Norway. But then, o' course, after we increased our production, we didn't need to git any from over there. Down at the new factory they make flake ice, but we never did –

it's a more modern process, yuh see. Another thing is that they only have about half-a-dozen people work there, where in the old days we had quite a lot o' employees. Yeah, we had three men to the engine-room on the three shifts and three on relief; there was two carpenters, a cooper, who made all the kits, four fitters and generally a boy with 'em, a painter, two cranemen, a foreman on the ice-floor with three men under him and three men on each o' the four wherries. Oh yeah, and two blokes on the lorries. Nowadays, at the new place, there's only one man in the engine-room, one craneman and about four blokes on the floor. Everything's altered. They don't need lorries of their own because the ice go straight over the market road in that elevator thing down into the trawlers. Or else the merchants' lorries pull up under the shute to load their kits up.

"One interestin' thing about the old place was that the company had once sunk their own well. Yeah, they did it a long time afore I got there. One o' the directors was a man named Mills and he'd made his money out in South Africa, in the gold mines. He had this well sunk so they wouldn't have to pay for mains water, and that went down somethin' like 1,800 foot – or so people reckoned. When they struck the water, it smelt like rotten eggs and couldn't be used for ice. But ol' Mr. Mills was a great believer in it for health reasons and he tried to sell it to the town as spa water. The Corporation wouldn't have nothin' to do with it, though he drank it himself. Yeah, and another thing he had done was git the carpenter to make a big, long trough, all divided up into compartments. In one he had brass, in the next one he had iron, in the next one tin, and in the next one zinc. He even had silver and gold. And all the compartments were padlocked up. The water used to run through the trough and over those elements for so long, then he'd have 'em all taken out and analysed. He reckoned there was radium in the water, but nothin' ever came of it. I drunk it myself for a year, but I didn't feel any better. That borehole was runnin' nearly all the time I worked at the old factory (the water used to run away down into the harbour); then about five or six years before we moved to the new place, it all caved in at the top."

Even if Mr. Mills's attempt to re-establish Lowestoft as a health resort failed (the town had been a modest spa in Georgian times), at least one other of the company's attempts at diversification succeeded. At the end of 1932 its managing director, W. F. Cockrell, enquired of the Richards shipbuilding firm concerning the possibility of constructing a new type of diesel trawler. Sidney Richards got busy on his drawing board and the Ala class began to emerge, 75 foot specialist near-water boats with Ruston-Hornsby engines. So impressed was Fred Cockrell with the designs that he placed an order for 12 of the vessels and set up a company called LT 1934 Ltd. to commemorate the building of the first one. In the event, the trawlers were always referred to as "the Ice Company boats" and seven in all were built before the Second World War broke out and brought things to a halt. The *Ala* (LT 347) was the prototype and she was followed by the *Eta* (LT 57), the *Willa* (LT 33), the *Gula* (LT 179), the *Rotha* (LT 208), the *Rewga* (LT 234) and the *Celita* (LT 236). They were excellent ships and good money-earners, and three of them have survived to the time of writing (1986). The *Gula*, the *Rotha* and the *Celita* no longer go trawling, but they are giving good service as gas-rig standby vessels.

Lowestoft inner harbour during a freeze-up of the 1890s, with the hulk of a sailing drifter in the foreground. It was during winters such as this one that ice was hacked from Lake Lothing and used in the local trawlfish industry. (Courtesy Jack Rose)

CHAPTER TEN

Net Making And Mending

'A millere was ther dwellynge many a day.
As any pecok he was proud and gay.
Pipen he coude and fisshe, and nettes bete,
And turne coppes, and wel both wrastle and sheete.'
('The Reeve's Tale' – Geoffrey Chaucer)

Early in the 19th century James Paterson invented a machine loom for producing cotton drift nets and, in 1820, set up a factory at Musselburgh. It was an event of great importance, and when Walter Ritchie of Leith perfected a mechanical means of tightening the knots the cotton drift net, or Scotch net as it became known, soon showed its superiority over the twine variety. It had two great advantages over the older 'rough' nets: it caught herrings more effectively and, being lighter, a boat could carry a greater number. Thus the vessel's catching power was increased and cotton drift nets became more and more widely used, until by the beginning of the 20th century they were almost universal. By then Musselburgh had become well-established as a centre of fishing-net manufacture, with a number of firms involved. At first these had agents or sales officers in other ports, but some eventually set up manufacturing branches. One such company, Stuart & Jacks, opened up in Lowestoft and Minnie Pitcher (born 1905) worked at their factory.

"I started work in 1919. There was quite a large family of us – two boys and four girls – and, o' course, in those days the mothers liked to give the sons a trade because they thought that they needed it. But not the girls. No, the girls went to work to help keep the boys. See, my brothers only got 2s. 6d. (12½p) a week when they first started their apprenticeships. Well, Mother couldn't afford to keep them on just that, so the girls had to help out. I went to the Stuart & Jacks net factory in Clapham Road and I started there at 7s. 6d. (37½p) a week. That was a kind of a trade too, I suppose, because it was beating. My mother and aunts had all worked at the factory and my mother went to see the foreman to get me in. In fact, all us girls, all four, worked there at one time or another and one o' my aunts was there at the same time too. She could tell yuh what any sort o' cotton was just by feeling it. My father worked for Craske's, deliverin' coal. He worked a 12 hour day for 18 shillins (90p) a week and, when we were little, we had to be in bed by the time he came home – which was six o' clock.

"The house we lived in was in Stevens Street. It had four bedrooms, which was a very good thing even though they were small, and there was a passage downstairs that came in very handy as well. See, when we were young, my mother used to take in Scotch girls to help make ends meet. She used to clear a room out for them downstairs and they used to bring all their things with them in a great big box. They used to wear oilies and boots for work and they used to take them orf outside in the passage and leave 'em there. When they didn't have any work to do, they used to go out round the town, knitting. That's the way

Mother used to rig us children out for the winter, takin' them in. Yes, she'd buy our boots or shoes or whatever we needed out o' that money.

"We worked a five and a half day week at the factory. Yes, it was 48 hours altogether, though if we were extra busy we would go from seven in the morning till seven at night. We got some overtime then, o' course. Sometimes, in the summertime, we were on shifts – six till two and two till ten – and that was done in order to get the nets out for the Home Fishing. There was no clocking in, but if you were a few minutes late for work in the morning the gates would be locked by the time you got there. No work that day! Oh, many's the time we've all been running along the road (see, there were the four of us girls all working there at the same time), because we weren't very good at getting up. There used to be a cripple lady in a shop near where we lived and she used to say, 'Oh, my goodness, look at all you running to work!'

"There was no time-wasting in the factory once you got there, either. No, there were no tea breaks or anything like that. We used to sneak a bit of lunch in, but it had to be done on the quiet. We just got an hour for dinner, and that was all. You were there to work and you had to work all the time. The conditions were fairly reasonable, but you did have to do what you were told. After I'd been there a few months, there was a rumour going round that our money was going up to 16 shillings (80p) a week. And I went home and told Mother. She said, 'I'll believe that when you bring it home.' But we did get it! It must have been when the Board of Trade started looking at wages after the First World War. Things began to get a little better then for poor people, because before that there really had been rich and poor. I worked at Stuart & Jacks from 1919 till 1927 and then I did beating at home for the Low'stoft Steam Herring Drifter Co. They had a net store on Whitney Green, at Pakefield, and I used to get between five shillins (25p) and 7s. 6d. (37½p) a net. I used to work outside in the summer and indoors when the weather was bad."

"At the factory we were working on new nets, made on the looms, but before you got to that you had to be taught certain things on just a piece o' net. All the nets came to the beatsters straight from the machines, to be examined and have any breaks in the cotton mended. The herring nets were the most important thing and they came off the machines in the correct sizes. Then, after they'd been inspected, they would be sent down the shute to the stretching room and be stretched to the exact length for the knots to be tightened. After that they used to go to a large shed at the back of the building to be guarded. That was the term we used for joining a strengthening piece o' net, made of thicker cotton, all the way down the sides. The next thing was for the net to be mounted, which meant putting cord right the way round all properly beated on with needles, after which young girls would put the ossels on. The nets went down to the tannery then, where the men added all the final ropes and tanned everything ready to send out. Not everything was done like that, though, because we did send a certain number o' lints out untreated. They were white, just as they came off the machine, and they were baled up after stretching. There was a press which they used to be put in, then they were stitched up in hessian ready to be sent away. A lot o' the export orders were done like that.

"To be a good beatster, you'd have to do a year's training. You started off on pieces o' net, learning to mend and all that, and then after about six months you went as an improver. That meant you went from the beating room to learn how to do the guarding and the mounting – and after another six months o' that you were a qualified beatster. O' course, some were quicker than others at picking it up. When we repaired, we used a small knife and a beatster's needle. They were bone ones usually, the needles – but when we did sardine nets we had little wooden ones. We were known as menders at the factory. Oh yes, we reckoned we were a bit above an ordinary beatster who worked on the store! You see, our work was absolutely clean. All the cotton was white, so we didn't get dirty. Oh, I enjoyed the work really.

"The cotton used to come in skeins and it went straight into the winding room. There were frames in there, like those wool-winding things you see, and it was put onto them and wound onto spools ready for the machines. There were all different thicknesses and qualities, o' course, and some o' the stuff was very good. Sea Island cotton was about the best and very expensive too, even in those days, and we used Egyptian and American cotton as well. The girls that started work in the winding room used to go on the machines when they got older. See, the cotton used to be taken through from the winding room to the machines, so those girls went automatically onto the machines as well. The little girls who used to put the *ossels* on, they'd mostly end up as mounters – you know, the ones that put the twine all the way round the net after it had been guarded.

"Us menders always had a bit of rivalry with the machinists. I don't know whether this was because any complaints made regarding the nets came from us, or whether we thought we were a bit more refined because the machinists had to shout their conversations at each other over the noise o' the machines. Then there were the mechanics. They were men, o' course, and they kept the machines in good order and saw to any breakdowns. When that happened the cotton would sometimes break and leave a big hole in the net. It was up to us to put that right then. Another thing we had to do was cut out any bits with oil on and replace them. Sometimes a loom would go wrong and the meshes would all be the wrong size. Well, we had to cut that whole piece out and replace it. The job was quite an important one, really.

"There was a charge-hand in each department and then a foreman over everything. The workers kept to their own departments because the toilets were on the workrooms, so it seemed to make a reserved atmosphere. There were ten qualified beatsters in our room, who worked on the regular orders, and then there were various numbers of apprentices according to net demand. If orders were plentiful, other beatsters were set on temporarily, though the firm wasn't very keen on setting outside beatsters on because their work wasn't always as good as ours. Our work had to be perfect to fit in with the net coming orf the machine, whereas the outsiders were probably used to their own kind o' work that they'd done on the store. Us beatsters (menders, I should say) worked in a long room, with hooks all down the walls on either side. It was above the stretching room, where the nets were stretched by machine after they came orf the loom. Only two people worked in there.

"Most o' the girls who started at the factory after leaving school used to keep there till they were married. No, there wasn't much turnover of staff. I mean, I stopped there until I was married, and there was even quite a few o' the older beatsters who stopped on. You were on your feet all the while, o' course. Yes, the beating was all done standing, and most of it was done in natural daylight where possible. We had the lights on in winter, but there was a glass roof to give you plenty o' daylight during normal hours. The only time you could sit down to work was when two pieces o' net had to be joined together. The work was all on the same level then and you could sit yourself down to do it."

A herring lint came off the loom at 55 yards length by 14 depth. Once it was set within its rope frame the length came down to 35 yards – what was called 'setting in by the third' – and it was this adjustment that gave the meshes their diagonal shape and allowed the net to hang correctly in the water. The Stuart & Jacks factory made many other kinds of fishing net as well and had an outstanding reputation for the quality of its products.

"The work had to be of a high standard right throughout the factory. My eldest sister was on a loom, I had one sister in the winding room, and the other two of us were beatsters. One thing I used to do was cut pieces out o' the various types o' net made and send them as samples to all the different customers. I would get the net that they wanted and cut off a piece so that they could actually see the size o' the mesh and everything. The sample was about two foot square and it used to be put in an envelope and get posted off. We used to send them out all over the world more or less. Oh, we weren't just tied to the Low'stoft fishing or the Scotch fishing. I mean, we did supply a lot o' local firms with herring nets and we sent a lot to Scotland, but we were busy all the year round doin' other things as well.

"We did quite a bit o' braiding. That was for cod nets and things, which mainly went abroad to foreign countries. Norway was quite a big customer. Oh yes, we used to braid up the different pieces for trawl nets (the cod end and the wings) and put them on. They couldn't make those on the looms, you see, so they all had to be braided by hand. We did seine nets as well, and most o' them used to go abroad. So did the sardine nets. They were a big order and they kept us goin' at the factory a lot o' the while. The only trouble with them was that the mesh was very small and it was hard to set the knots. Somebody would have to specially look at them and make sure that they were properly tied. See, if the knots weren't tight, the meshes would slip all over the place. Sometimes the sardine nets used to be sent back to us and they'd have to be re-done. We never got herring nets comin' back; it was always the sardines."

The net-making factories in Lowestoft have long disappeared, but a considerable number of the boat-owning companies' former beating chambers still survive, though they have mainly been converted to other uses. All have a distinctive rectangular shape and usually stand two storeys high, with the upper floor providing the working space for the beatsters themselves and the lower one being utilised for the storage of fishing gear. The word "beatster" itself derives from an old English word "beat" or "bete", which means to mend or make good. Two notable and early instances of its use in literature occur in the late 14th century. Chaucer uses it in the 'Reeve's Tale', where the miller of Trumpington is being described, and it also crops up in the second Wycliffe Bible in the Gospel account of James and John being called to discipleship. Mary Fisk (born 1896) inherited the word as her job description over 500 years later, when she began work in a net-store not far from her home in Pakefield.

"I come from a fishin' family. My father was chief engineer on the *Incentive* (LT 581), which belonged to the Harvey family o' Kessingland. He got drowned at Shields in 1912. They were comin' up from Lerwick and they used to fish on the way home and stop at all the different ports. When we were little, he used to bring us children some Scarborough rock home and we all thought that was marvellous. The way he got drowned was that he'd been ashore and was comin' back to the boat, when he missed his footin' and fell. He probably fell down between the dock wall and the boat, struck his head and drowned. My mother and one o' my sisters had to go right down to Shields to identify him. There were five children in the fam'ly. My brother was the oldest, then there were four girls. I was already out at work as a beatster and there was only one younger'n me, so things weren't too bad – not really.

"My mother used to do nursin'. When women had babies, Mother would go out and nurse them while they were poorly. Oh yes, she used to go out right into the country. I can picture people now, comin' after her in pony and traps. She had one o' those straw portmanteau things with a lid and she kept all her stuff in that. She never worked without a doctor, though. Before she was married Mother was a servant in Low'stoft, and the lady who she worked for wanted to pay for her to have tuition at the hospital to learn to be a nurse. She never did train, but she always had that way with her. Yeah, and she was allus glad to be on the go to earn a little extra money. Oh, she did work hard, Mother did, and she died very suddenly when she was only 56. I thought the world o' my mum.

"I actually started beatin' for the County Fishing Company at their store in The Avenue. I was about 14½ when I began there and my money was only about 1s 6d or two shillins (7½ or 10p) a week. After you'd qualified as a beatster, which took about a year to 18 months, the money went up. I think I got about eight shillin's (40p) a week when I came out o' my time. We used to work till nine o' clock at night durin' the Home Fishin', but we got overtime pay for it after a certain time. We worked Saturday mornins as well and there were no regular holidays, apart from just one or two bank holiday days. After Christmas we used to get stood orf and there was no dole or anything to come. We just had to be laid orf until there was the work to do again with the Scotch voyage comin' on.

"When you first started at the job, you'd gotta learn how to mend holes in the nets and how to cut pieces out and put pieces in. You got what were called spoilt nets comin' into the store and they'd all got to be repaired. O' course, the more you learnt, the quicker you got at the job, until you were ready to come out o' your time. We used to do mackerel nets as well as the herrin' lints. They had the great flat corks on 'em, not the round ones with holes in, but the latter part o' the time they became more or less like a Scotch net. I carried on as a beatster when I married my husband, in 1926, because he never earnt a lot o' money as a fisherman. He went herrin' catchin' in the *Osprey* (LT 1076) for Mr. Tiddley Catchpole and his money was 16s 8d (83p) a week. That used to be sent to me by the firm, but it used to be taken orf the earnins at the end o' the voyage. After we got married, we had to get out o' our house in Pakefield because the landlord wanted it for his daughter, so we went to live in Kessingland. I worked as a beatster, just the same. Yes, I worked for Boiler Tripp and for Arthur Billy Harvey as well. I even mended sprat nets durin' the time I lived in Kessingland. Poor ol' Hundred Catchpole used to have 'em and they'd got a very small mesh.

"After a time I started work for Jack Breach on the Kittiwake Store. That was on Battery Green Road in Low'stoft, where Marks and Spencer's car park now is. I used to go down on the eight o' clock bus every day, then catch the half-past four one hoom. That was the hours we worked, with just a half-hour for dinner. They were very particular about the work you did at Breach's. When you put a bit o' lint in a net, you had to split all the knots so the job looked all nice and neat and tidy. Yes, you'd think it was the original net when you'd done. You used a little beatin' knife to split with and you normally held it in your left hand as you worked, just to click the ends o' the cotton orf. When you cut a bad piece o' net out, you'd use your right hand. There was a forewoman on the store and you could go and ask her opinion about a bad tear in a net – you know, whether to pick the ends up or to put a new piece in. Some o' the nets used to have great big holes in sometimes. We used to call 'em cod's chaps. Dogfish used to do the worst damage. They'd tear the net to bits. Yes, you couldn't do nothin' with 'em, so you'd have to cut the whole net right out o' the frame and put a new lint in. The old one used to go for garden lint then.

'We used two kinds o' cotton as we worked. There was a thick one for the sides and the headings and a finer one for mendin' the mashes. We had wooden blades to put the skeins o' cotton on and you used to fill your needles orf them. There used to be a rumpus if someone took the last o' the cotton orf a blade and never put a new lot on! As well as repairin' nets, we used to git the lints comin' in from the factory and make them up. That was hard work. We had to half-hitch all the way round the cords at so many knots to the foot and we used to put the *norsels* on. The men used to do the final settin' up, puttin' all the ropes and corks on, o' course. Sometimes the lints were white when they came to us and sometimes they were already tanned. It all depended on what'd been done at the net factory. I have made the wings and cod ends on trawl nets and durin' the war I braided up camouflage nets with one o' the big wooden needles. What I didn't like was mendin' nets what'd had jellyfish in 'em. They used to sting us, even though the nets were dry. You could feel it for a long while afterwards. Right through your clothes it used to go, a sort of an old dust. That used to make your lips sore as well and some o' the girls even put tissues up their noses to stop breathin' it in.

"We got paid by the week at Breach's and we used to go in Saturday mornins as well. But then the latter part o' the time it got so that everyone finished on the Friday night. I never got stood orf at Breach's. There was always so many boats in the firm that there was plenty o' work. After the war I did nets at home. They used to leave me two nets at a time, though sometimes I'd have three, and they'd bring me the money I'd earnt as well. I didn't have to go after it; it was all done in little envelopes. I got about ten bob (50p) a net and that came in very handy.

"When you look back on it all now, it seems marvellous to think that there's no beatin' any more. It makes yuh wonder where the herrin' have all gone, don't it?"

Beatsters and braiders at work at a Lowestoft net-store during the 1940s. The fine-meshed herring nets can hardly be seen (note the cork-line, however, between the two women nearest the camera), but the larger, coarser trawl sections are plainly visible. (Courtesy Jack Rose)

CHAPTER ELEVEN

Baskets Galore

'Oh, the willow tree will twist
And the willow tree will twine.
I wish I did lie in a young man's arms
That once had this heart of mine.'
('The Seeds Of Love – traditional)

The use of baskets both on board ship and on the quayside has long been part of the fishing industry and with considerable areas of river-marsh in their immediate hinterlands, both Lowestoft and Great Yarmouth had no touble in getting hold of suitable raw materials for their basketmakers to work upon. This ground was systematically planted and cropped on coppice principles.

The Great Yarmouth firm of Stanley Bird (Basketware) Ltd. once drew its living mainly from fishing, but now produces goods for numerous other uses. Its craftsmen make items as diverse as cane furniture, Ali Baba linen baskets, hot-air balloon gondolas, stage props, frames for the Guards Regiments' busby helmets, the Queen Mother's dog baskets, wheel-around bulk bins for mail-order firms, and bird-cages, as well as shopping baskets. Much of the willow used now comes from the Parrett marshes in Somerset because local supplies are no longer sufficient to meet the demand. However, Stanley Bird (born 1917) remembers when most of the trade depended on the fishing industry.

"My grandfather first started the business in about 1860. He was a Yarmouth man, but he wasn't a basketmaker by trade, No, he'd done all sorts o' things – he went to sea and he'd been a bricklayer. Then, when he was in his twenties, he started doin' baskets. He used to put a pile of 'em on his head and go down to the Fish Market and sell 'em. He got a few orders to start with, then more and more, and that was how he built the business up. As his boys got older, they all went inta the business with him, and some of 'em were good basketmakers and some weren't so good. My father was the youngest one in the family and, o' course, he wasn't such a good basketmaker. He was a good man for the trade in other ways. I started orf when I left school at 14 and I've done over 50 years in the trade, exceptin' for the time I was in the forces durin' the war. When I first started orf, my father used to let me help him run the business. Yeah, I used to go to the bank and git the men's wages and I also went round to see people and git orders.

"A lot o' the willow we use now come from Somerset, but in the old days we got the stuff from Norfolk. My grandfather had beds out at Caister and, when I was a boy, I remember us havin' some at Martham and Winterton. They were hirin' grounds; we used to lease the land for a period o' years. After the Second World War we bought the grounds here in Burgh Castle and started growin' osiers on them. 1947 was the year we began that. I've also got a workshop place in Runham Vauxhall and that's been in the family now for over 100 years. Growin' willows isn't very straightforward, you know. No, there's a lot hang to it. In fact, if you could be sure of gittin' willows regular and all the while, you'd be best to buy 'em. It's no cheaper to grow 'em. No. The only thing is that you have so much trouble gittin' hold of everything you want that you hafta grow a certain amount.

"Now, willows and osiers are different, you see. Round here we can grow a good osier, but down in Somerset they grow good willow. It's the climate that does it. See, they git four or five months' warmth down there, where we're lucky if we git three. If you git hold of a willow and cut it, you'll find that there's only a very little pith, but if you cut an osier you'll find that there's more pith than outside wood. Willows are grown on pollards, rather like the shape o' your fist, and they're kept like that all the while. I doubt very much if they git to three feet high in twenty year. An osier is a bigger, rougher tree. That grows out at the sides a lot more if you leave it. We like to keep 'em as short as we can, but after a time they begin to grow right out and have to be grubbed up. Both willows and osiers begin to deteriorate after about ten or fifteen year. Yeah, I mean, the first year after you've put the new sets in, I suppose you get about three wands four or five foot long. The next year you git six or seven orf each set, praps five, or six or seven foot long. The year after that you'll git the same length, only double the amount. Then, in the fourth year, you begin to come inta the prime and you'll probably be liftin' somethin' like seven ton an acre.

"When we grow the osiers here at Burgh Castle, the land is ploughed up and limed. You don't need a lot o' manure, but the ground has to be limed so it isn't sour. The best way is to git it ready and leave it for three or four months before puttin' the sets in. You plant out in March and start cuttin' the wands in December. We finish cuttin' about the end o' February and everything is sorted out into sizes and qualities. After that the bundles are stood in about four inches o' water so they start to re-grow. We've got a dyke all specially dammed up for that. Once they come out in leaf, they're put through a machine to strip the bark orf. We used to do 'em by hand at one time, but you can't git the women now to do it so we do 'em by machine. Once the bark is orf, that leaves a nice white wood. The wands are dried then – stowed away and kept for a year. When they're brought out to be used they're put in a little drop o' water for about four hours, just to moisten 'em up for workin' with. You do the same wi' willows, only they don't need so much water as the osiers.

"We can git seven, eight, nine and even ten foot lengths orf our oisiers; and as long as I can buy five and six foot Somerset willows, then I'm all right. There's a big demand for them two sizes, you see. You know how shoppin' baskets are a brown colour? – well, you git that by boilin' the willows. They're dried out with the bark still on, then put into a tank and boiled for eight hours. The dye out o' the bark goes into the willow rod itself, so when the bark is stripped orf the colour is there. You can boil osiers as well. Oh yeah. The only thing is that the small ones aren't worth it because they're nearly all pith. The big ones are all right, though, and we do a lot o' them. We used to git big willows at one time from The Argentine, but the market's dried up now because they need what they produce for themselves. There used to be a lot o' osiers grown down at Wickham Market, but that's another thing what's gone. Ol' Mullins used to be the basketmaker down there and it's his machine what we've got here at Burgh for strippin' with.

"Osiers and willows do the same job really, but there's certain things that we like to keep 'em for. Take a square delivery basket, for example – well, the sides are willow, but the uprights are osier because they won't stand so much bendin'. Now, you could make the whole thing out o' osier if you went slow and steady, but the men don't like that because they're on piecework. They want quick boughs, which means the willow because it never breaks. No, it never breaks, where an osier is liable to if you're a bit harsh with it. We use osiers on round baskets because there isn't the bendin' round corners like there is on the square work. Once you start doin' that, you really want willow. The only trouble is that our climate here is a bad one for growin' willows, so osier is a second best sort o' thing. That looks nice, though, as regards colour. Oh yeah. I mean, if you had two baskets beside you, one willow and one osier, nine times out o' ten people would pick the osier one out because it looked nicer. Somerset willow is good quality stuff, but the colour isn't as good as the osier's.

"We use a lot o' cane in our baskets as well. All the best stuff comes from Indonesia; the Malaysian cane is a bit harder and not so good to work with. I spose we use about half a ton a week nowadays, but that used to be a ton at one time with all the fishin' baskets we made. On the quarter-cran baskets there were cane handles, a cane ridge round the inside and cane right round the bottom. That was put where the baskets had gotta be strong. Cane is strong, you see, and that'll stand all the wet you like to give it. Just the same with willow. Yeah, all willow and cane stuff needs to stand out in the rain. Anything you've got in the basket line needs to be out in the rain. It won't take no harm. It grow in the water, don't it? People will keep baskets dry, so eventually they git brittle. They wanta put 'em out in the rain for a little while! If we've got anything in the shop which we've had in there for a while, we think, 'Oh, that wants freshin' up.' So we put it out in the rain and leave it there. It looks lovely, comes up like new again.

"As regards trainin', it's best to git boys straight out o' school. Yeah, I like to git 'em when they're young so they don't know another job at all. Once they've been in another job, they're not so good to go into basketmakin'. The apprenticeship is still about five years, which is what it always used to be if you made swills and baskets. If you made swills alone, that was three years. I never done a proper apprenticeship myself; I just started straight into the business. I've got the indentures for a man who started work in 1925 and he got five shillings (25p) a week for the first year, 7s. 6d (37½p) for the second, ten shillins (50p) for the third, and then half-pay for the fourth and fifth year. I spose a man would ha' been earnin' about two pound a week in them days, so he probably got a pound as half-pay.

"Afore the war we could only take on one apprentice for every so many men employed. That was a rule laid down by the Basketmakers Union, but that don't apply today. We don't really sign apprentices now, anyway. No, we take 'em on as trainees and teach 'em the trade. As soon as they can make baskets, we pay 'em a rate for the job and let 'em git started. That encourages 'em to be quick, because if they haven't got the speed they aren't goin' to be no good to themselves or anyone else. That don't matter about doin' the work perfect to start with; that'll come wi' practice. The main thing to look out for is speed. Afore the war the apprentices used to start straight away on baskets. Oh yes, there was no messin' about! Even today, if you can't manage it the first day, you git 'em onta baskets on the second. That you do. And within a week or two they're proba'ly makin' one particular type. Oh, we git 'em on what we call the *plank* as soon as we can.

"Our men used to work ten or eleven hours a day, where it's down to about eight or nine today, and they'd work Saturdays as well. Nowadays the men can please themselves whether they come in on Saturday mornins or not, and they can also start and finish when they like durin' the week. Praps some of 'em like to git in at seven in the mornin' and knock orf at four, where others will start at eight and finish about five. See, they're all on piecework, so they can come and go as they like. They've all got keys to our main place in King Street. In the old days we always used to do the tanks on a Saturday mornin' – you know, take the wands out o' the water and fill 'em up again for the next week. The stuff takes longer to soak in the winter because o' the cold weather. Yeah, that wants about a fortnight then, where a week is enough durin' the summer. This is stuff with the bark still on that I'm talkin' about. If the bark is orf, then four hours is usually enough.

"A good basketmaker used to be able to make about 25 swills a week and he got 2s 2d (11p) for each one. With the quarter-crans the men would do about six or seven a day at 1s 9d (8½p) a go. O' course, you got people slower than that and you got ones who were quicker. Nowadays a good basketmaker can earn up to £150 a week. In the old days the summer used to be our busy time, gittin' ready for the autumn fishin'. Durin' the winter, when things were a bit slack, the men would go out inta the country to cut willows. They were happy to be kept busy. You can't do that today, o' course – a basketmaker is a basketmaker – so we git somebody else to do the cuttin'. And another thing – that wouldn't really pay us today to have the men out for about three months, cuttin' osiers and willows, because while they were doin' that they wouldn't be makin' anything. We need them producin' stuff five days a week in order to make the business pay. I did try women as basketmakers after the war. Yeah, I had nine or ten of 'em, but that wasn't successful. They weren't strong enough to do the heavy work involved. No, they couldn't make their money on piecework. They found that they could earn more in the factories in Yarmouth with about half the amount o' work."

Making ready for the autumn herring season or 'Home Fishing' as it was always known was the most important time in the basketmakers year. During the months of October, November and December Great Yarmouth was the largest and busiest herring port in the world, packed with Scottish fishermen and itinerant shoreworkers. An often quoted figure is the thousand drifter fleet which worked out of the town. This was largely comprised of vessels from north of the border (742 out of 1006 in 1913, 973 out of 1179 in 1920), and it was their presence in town which largely accounted for the fish wharves being covered with that unique and most distinctive of Yarmouth's fish containers, the *swill* basket referred to earlier. It was a large, oblong-shaped wicker affair, with a bar handle across its middle, and it held about two-thirds of a cran of herring.

"In the old days that was all fishin' where we were concerned. We used to turn nearly everything else away. We were workin' just for Yarmouth then. We never done nothin' for Low'stoft. The main thing was fishin' baskets for the herrin', though when I came out o' the forces after the last war we started to do quite a lot o' trade baskets. Swills were the thing at one time, o' course. Yeah, we'd have praps ten men make about 10,000 o' them for the Hoom Fishin' and we'd do a certain number o' quarter-crans as well. With the swills you'd start at the top o' the basket and work downwards, but with the quarter-crans that was the other way about: you'd work from the bottom and come upwards. The swills were mainly made from osier, with a certain amount o' hazel in 'em. Yeah, ordinary hazel, three or four year old. We used to git ours from woods owned by people like Lord Somerleyton and the Duke o' Norfolk. What we wanted was dead straight stuff, six foot long. The other bits used to go for thatchin' *brotches*. There used to be 60 hazels to the bunch and we'd have several thousand bunches each year. The idea o' usin' it was for strength – well, and cheapness as well, because hazel wasn't very dear in them days.

"All the swills used to be painted with the marks o' the different firms they belonged to. They used to give us the paint and we did the markin' for 'em. For instance, the Northern Fishin' Company o' Peterhead had a white N on a black background. There used to be dumps for 'em at the back o' the Fish Market – you know, bits o' land where they could all be put. Them places are all built over now and used by the oil firms. Durin' the winter a lot o' the swills would want mendin', so we used to do repair work for all the various people. A lot o' the Scotch firms had their places down on the fish wharf and they used to give us the keys to look after for 'em. Yeah, we'd work in them places as if they were our own and we'd keep an eye on everything till they wanted the premises again about the end o' August. That was so they could start to git ready for The Fishin' again. Swills were still in use right up till the middle 50s, but by that time the herrin' was dyin' out.

"Before the war the swills used to cost about five bob (25p) each and they'd last about three years. After that they were chucked away and burned up. Today a swill (people have 'em for log baskets) would cost about £35. Yeah, if there was herrins about today, swills wouldn't be used because they'd be too dear. A quarter-cran basket was about half-a-crown (12½p) or three bob (15p), where nowadays that'd set yuh back £17.50. All our quarter-crans had to be inspected and branded by the Weights and Measures people about every week or fortnight. Everything had gotta be just right and made to the correct specification. After a while the baskets used to stretch and the Weights and Measures inspector would go down onta the Fish Market and condemn any he found what weren't up to the mark.

"Our labour force today is about 20 people. When I first started, that was eight or nine – though we'd set extra men on if we needed 'em. Oh yeah, we employ more people now, with all the different things we make. And another thing – where a man done about six or seven baskets a day afore the war, he'll do praps ten or a dozen now. They're not quite so well made proba'ly, but they're good enough. I spose a basketmaker come inta his prime when he's about 25 or 26, and by the time he's 30 he can do anything. That's just as well we've got all these other things to make because fishin' died away in Yarmouth very quickly. Yeah, the Scotch fleet went down and down and the fishin' went with it. And yet I can remember the time when a lot o' the fields out here at Burgh were manured with herrins. The farmers used to buy 'em at about sixpence (2½p) a cran and spread 'em on the fields. That was back before the war, when they were dumpin' 'em because there was too many on the market. Lovely herrin' they were as well! It's a great pity when you think of all that good food goin' to waste."

That sentiment would be re-echoed by many people, but there is no setting the clock back. Recent years have seen the reopening of the North Sea herring fishing after a long period of prohibition imposed by the EEC authorities, but the number of boats involved each autumn has been few. The drifters have all gone and, with them, most of the expertise built up over generations. There is no real sale for large quantities of herring either, and there probably won't be until one of the giant food-processing firms decides to present the fish in a convenient form to the modern housewife. Though the Yarmouth Port And Haven Commissioners have bravely declared their faith in the future by investing in a new fish wharf on the Gorleston side of the river, it is doubtful whether the herring will ever again become a major part of the town's economy. However, Stanley Bird's firm still retains its traditional links with fishing in a variety of products – though often with customers a long way from Great Yarmouth.

"Nowadays we do a lot o' work for fishin' ports all over the place. Yeah, I mean our baskets even go as far as St. John's, in Newfoundland. We've got a several Scottish customers, o' course, and some of 'em go right back to my grandfather's time. Oh, we supply Aberdeen, Lerwick, Kinlochbervie, the Hebrides and the Isle o' Lewis, Mallaig – all o' them. And Ireland – northern and southern Ireland. The Isle o' Man, Fleetwood, Milford Haven, Swansea. Then there's Newlyn and Plymouth and Brixham. We send a lot direct to Cosalt at Brixham and that's part o' the business which has been built up since the war. We supply Grimsby through that firm as well and our stuff also git down to Whitby. Along the Essex coast there's Maldon and all them places, right down as far as Southend, and then locally there's Low'stoft. Yeah, we do a lot o' stuff for Low'stoft these days.

"Now, it's a funny thing, but the Yarmouth quarter-cran used to be a heavier basket than the Low'stoft one. I don't know why; it's just the way it was. Oh, I could tell a Low'stoft quarter-cran from a Yarmouth one straight away! Mr. Daines did all the Low'stoft quarter-crans at one time. I knew him, and when he finished I took his trade over. In fact, towards the end o' his time we were supplyin' him. Another thing is the differences in the fish baskets used on board trawlers. The Low'stoft ones are 75 pounders, where the Grimsby ones are 100. Then you git other kinds o' variation, like North Shields has an oval type with four handles and Aberdeen has the same shape but with two handles. All the different places have their own little things by which you tell 'em. You can see it in the work as well. I mean, like I said, I could always tell a Low'stoft quarter-cran from a Yarmouth one. And I could tell Hull work from Aberdeen work. Oh, you got to know. That was the way the baskets were made that did it; you know, the way the osiers or the willows were laid. I mean, it's just the same with the men who work for our firm. I can tell yuh which o' them has made a particular basket. Yeah, it's the way the thing has been done. Every man has got his own way."

The wooden steam drifter *Golden Spur*, built by John Chambers in 1908 – untypical in that most boats by then had their wheel-houses foreside of the funnel. This vessel caught fire and sank off Scarborough on September 11th, 1926, luckily, without any loss of life.

CHAPTER TWELVE

Building Drifters

'So many a ship of peaceful purpose was called to the tasks of war,
Was manned and armed and made anew for work unguessed before.
Came quietly into the dockyard and, converted, slipped away:
Yacht, trawler, ferry, liner, tramp. So came the "Jervis Bay".'
('The Jervis Bay' – Michael Thwaites)

There are documentary records of ships being built on the beach at Lowestoft as far back as the middle of the 18th century, and it is likely that this work had been going on much longer than that. There was no harbour until the opening of the Lowestoft–Norwich Navigation in 1830. It was extended and improved by Samuel Morton Peto during the 1840s and then small shipbuilding yards began to spring up on the shores of Lake Lothing. This lagoon of brackish water, formerly separated from the sea by a shingle bar, had become the port's inner harbour and its sheltered margins were ideal for shipyards. Boats were required in larger numbers from mid-century onwards, as the coming of the railway increased the demand for fish. One of the most notable enterprises to be established was that of John Chambers Ltd., a flourishing firm with a yard on each side of Lowestoft's inner harbour and with a third at the western end of Lake Lothing, known as No. 3 yard. One man who worked on the No. 3 yard is Ted Frost (born 1901) who since his retirement has done a great service to maritime history by recording in his own book *From Tree To Sea* the detailed building of a classic steam drifter.

"I left Roman Hill School in July 1915 and I wanted to be a shipwright, because some o' my family were in that trade and my father was a sawyer on John Chambers' yard. There were a couple o' fishermen as well on the male side o' the family and, out o' the womenfolk, seven were beatsters. So you can see that we were always in the fishin' industry. When the First World War broke out, the Admiralty commandeered all suitable fishin' vessels for patrollin' and minesweepin', but building came to a standstill because nobody was certain o' what was goin' to be needed. That meant I couldn't get an apprenticeship, so I had to look round for somethin' else. I got a job first of all at Lawrence's ginger beer factory in Hervey Street, but I only stayed there about four days. I soon had enough o' that!

"The next thing I did was work for W. H. Smith & Son, deliverin' morning and evening papers and so on for five shillins (25p) a week. I got on very well indeed at that and I was given charge o' the Oulton Broad station bookstall after a while for an extra shillin' (5p) a week. Well, that was all right, except that I had to do a morning round o' papers and there were a lot o' dogs in the yards round Oulton Broad! I told Mr. Welton, the Low'stoft manager, that I didn't want the job any more, but that when I went back inta Low'stoft I wanted to keep that extra shillin'. He said he'd hafta see what W. H. said when he came down in a week or two's time. Well, W. H. did come down, in his frock coat, silk hat and straight trousers, and I was allowed to have the shillin'. So that was all right; that was fine.

"Eventually, though, another job came along which was worth 12 shillins (60p) a week, so I took it. That was down at Mr. Burwood's beatin' chamber in Ness Road, on The Beach, near the Low Light. I was cuttin' up rope for about 50 or so girls to make shell grommets from. Mr. Burwood himself cut up the big rope for the large shells and so on, while I cut up the smaller rope and *spunyarn* for the six inch, the 4.7s and that sort o' thing. I enjoyed doin' that immensely, and in addition to my wages I got a bit o' extra money from the sale o' all the odd rope ends and stuff to the people who dealt in that kind o' thing. In the end, though, my father came home one day and told me that I could start on John Chambers' Number Three yard at Oulton Broad, where he worked himself. The firm had decided that they were goin' to build some more drifters, so that gave a chance to lads like me to get started inta shipbuildin'. I actually began work there on the 26th o' April, 1916, which was the day after the bombardment o' Low'stoft. I'd been down on the front the previous day with some o' the boys, near the Royal Hotel, lookin' at the ships and watchin' the shells splash in the water. We could hear 'em goin' over the top of us as well and we just missed the one which blew up the house alongside the hotel.

"I went straight onta the yard and began to work on framin' wooden steam drifters. I can't remember the names o' the first ones I worked on, but later on we built the *Implacable* (LT 730) and the *Formidable* (LT 100) and those I remember very well. During 1918 we started to build wooden standard drifters and the place in which the first one was laid down still exists in Fletcher's Boatyard. Mr. William S. Parker designed the first wooden *standard drifter*. He was the yard designer on Number Three and a wonderful man at his job. So was Mr. Ernest Chambers, who was the designer on the Low'stoft yards. Those standard boats we built were an enlarged version of the Chambers 420 Class and we built several of 'em altogether on our yard, as well as fittin' out some o' the ones built at Low'stoft because the Low'stoft yards were so busy doin' repair work for The Admiralty. When the war ended and the buzz went round about it bein' over, nobody believed it! We all kept on workin', till it eventually sunk in that it really had finished. There were celebrations then. I remember the first thing I did was head for the Fish Market. Yeah, I headed orf down there and I remember seein' the little ol' *Ocean's Gift* (LT 387) discharging herrin' near the sale-ring.

"I used to walk into work from where I lived in Bevan Street, which was a distance of about one and a half miles, and then I often used to walk out inta the country from the yard. See, we felled our own timber and we had a traction engine and horses to shift it with. Two of us were detailed at three shillins (15p) a week extra to go out into the country with the tree-fellers to make sure that the timber was cut up suitably. The branches, or *wrongs* as we called 'em, were used to make the frames so they all had to be cut out properly for the sawmill. We took a mould with us to help do the job, because we used the bends and twists in the branches to get the shape o' the frames. All the timber was seasoned for a year, if possible, but quite often that'd be used green. We'd walk out to Mutford, Henstead, Hulver, Kessingland, Gisleham, but any further out and the work was left to local fellers. See, timber was taken in from about 15 to 20 miles from the yard.

"On the Chambers Number Three yard there about ten men in the sawmill, (includin' the labourers who carried the timber when the frames were bein' cut), nine or ten shipwrights, and eight or nine shipwright apprentices. In the blacksmith's shop there were three blacksmiths (four when the standard drifters were bein' built), three strikers and a driller. There was an engine driver to keep the machinery goin' and about four joiners and one apprentice in the joinery shop. We didn't have any painters, though; that work was done by an Oulton Broad firm, Mr. Bert Fuller's. He did all the plumbin' as well and his men were always around the yard. That was good work what they did too. Chambers did build engines. Yes, a certain number. They built the engine for *La Parisienne* (LT 213), a boat which they actually owned; she had a water-tube boiler in her, the only Low'stoft drifter ever to have one. Prior to 1910 the engineerin' workshops had belonged to Messrs. Davis of Poplar, London, but I can't tell you how many men worked in them. What I do know is that we only had a five ton crane on the yard, so the engines had to be fitted further down the harbour at the *sheer-legs crane*.

"Elliott & Garrood supplied all the capstans for the boats – except the standard drifters, which had a winch instead. At the time the *Formidable* was built, in 1917, there were nearly 6,000 o' them capstans in use all over the world and there were 21 different sizes. When there was a larnchin' everyone was a bit excited, but the day o' days as far as I'm concerned was the day when steam was raised and the engine turned over for the first time. That mornin' the boiler would be gittin' nice and hot and the paint would begin to burn. Well, what with that and the smell o' tar and varnish and all the rest of it, for me that was special. I never went out on any drifter trial trips, but I did go out once or twice on some little ol' ice-wherries what we built. I remember bein' right down orf Sparrow's Nest once and a destroyer came through the Stanford Channel. That was at the end o' the war, and this destroyer came past us and set up a terrific wash that nearly rolled us over. See, those little boats weren't really meant for the sea."

Lowestoft was an important naval base in both world wars for patrol vessels and minesweepers, many of which were converted steam drifters and trawlers. Their repair and conversion became important war work for several years, but during the First World War this naval activity resulted in an important innovation. This was the introduction of steel construction into the port. Until the Admiralty produced a specification for standard fishing vessels built of steel all local shipbuilding had been in wood.

"Durin' the First World War I should think that John Chambers maintained the bulk o' the minesweepers in Low'stoft. There was a special gang o' men workin' on them all the time, repairin' the *kites* and doin' repairs to the boats themselves. As I said earlier, we fitted out some o' the standard boats on the Number Three yard because the two Low'stoft yards were so busy with Admiralty work. I remember that I was workin' on one called the *Atmosphere* (GY 45) when the war ended and the armistice was signed. I spent quite a lot o' time fittin' guns onta standard drifters. See, they had a gun for'ad and the guns were usually Japanese. I spent many, many hours on Sundays drillin' holes for the ratchet and the drill post to fit gun pedestals down. All the boats had a monkey island on them, or a signal bridge as they used to call it, and they had winches fitted instead o' capstans.

"We put down guns on other fishin' craft that came to be armed – you know, besides the standard boats. And another thing I did was to fit depth charges and G-charges to some of 'em. They carried four depth charges, rigged up on a bracket right on the *taffrail*, and these would roll orf overboard one after the other. On the *quarters* were the two G-charges and they were fired out o' their cradles. I suppose it was done by an explosive charge. Bein' involved in that work resulted in me gittin' rides in one o' the fastest motor boats ever built up to that time, the *Baby 5*. She was used by the naval base and I went with Lieutenant Puttefoot down to the torpedo base in her. Oh, she was a fast boat. It was a real privilege to have a ride in her. There weren't many people who travelled in *Baby 5*!

"Towards the end o' the war one or two places started to build steel standard drifters. Colby's, over the other side o' the water, built the *Flash* (FD 379) in 1918. Shipwrights built her, even though she was a steel boat, but that was the only time it was done. After that platers and shipyard steel workers began to arrive, and when Brookes' Yard began to build there were several steel drifters about the place what were never used for war purposes. Chambers opened a steel-yard in 1920, I think it was, and one or two drifters were turned out, as well as a number o' coasters and various other vessels. Orders came in for them and quite a lot o' men came down from the North o' England and from Scotland to work in the yard. I made several friends among 'em, but we used to think they were a rough lot at first. We never could understand why they were so ragged, but once I started to work on steel ships I very soon found out! It was because they were always tearin' their clothes on jagged edges and that sort o' thing. And another thing – we'd always been used to hobnailed boots. Well, that wouldn't do on a steel ship either, especially if she was layin' on the yard. What with the declivity and the sheer, you'd soon be on down on your behind if you wore hobnailed boots!

"The workmanship in my time at John Chambers was pretty good. Everybody took a pride in their work. And the steel ships we built were, oh, fair. You'd never see anything more fair. They were beautiful! Oh, Chambers did turn out a good quality job, both in wood and steel. We built several ships with *Regis* in the name, coasters they were, about 800 tons – the *Royal Regis*, the *Salcombe Regis*, the *Melcombe Regis*. Mind you, the firm didn't make much money on them because the people they were buildin' them for got every penny's worth o' work done that they were capable of through careful readin' o' the contract. Chambers were very trustin' people and there was quite a lot o' fiddlin' on the yards just after the war. See, there was a bit of a boom on in shipbuildin' and people took advantage. For example, some o' the riveters used to work it so that they got paid twice for doin' just one lot o' rivets. Well, the firm couldn't stand that. When the boom began to fall away after a couple or three years, things were tightened up a bit – especially where the stores were concerned. Oh yeah, if you wanted anything, you had to see the chargehand and git a requisition slip for whatever was required.

"When the depression really set in, in the 1930s, the firm came to an end. It was closed down by the govern'ment through Shipyard Securities Ltd. Yeah, they were closin' shipyards right, left and centre, Just like Dr. Beechin' shut down the railway lines. 1931 was when it all came to an end and the Chambers family were out of a job. They were all involved in the business, always had been – except for Wilfrid, who was killed in the First World War. Charlie and Alan, the oldest and youngest, both worked in the yards, while Ernest was a designer. I'm not sure what Charlie did after the firm went bust, but Alan finished up in the book trade, while poor Ernest went erectin' fences. That upset everyone to think o' him doin' that. I'm not sayin' anything depreciatingly about anybody who puts fences up. I don't mean that at all. What I mean is that a man of his talent, a ship designer, should be forced inta that line o' work."

When John Chambers Ltd. ceased to trade, Ted Frost was at sea as a ship's carpenter and had, in fact, been doing the job for a number of years in both refrigerated meat ships to Argentine and in cargo vessels on the Pacific coast run. His affection for the establishment where he had learned his craft was undiminished, however, and has remained constant over the years. This feeling is not only due to the recognition of the value of working skills acquired on the No. 3 yard, but the result also of the good times experienced there. The atmosphere was a happy one, with a fair amount of practical joking and, in the best traditions of British industry, a lot of it was directed by older men at the young apprentices. Apart from the horseplay, though, there were also a number of social and sporting activities which took place and these added to the appeal of working for John Chambers.

"I've never worked in another environment such as obtained there. That was the happiest place I was ever in. O' course, the older men used to do some terrible things to the boys, but for some reason or other they were never done to me. I remember one occasion where two o' the apprentices, Siddy and Victor Tuttle, had a joke played on 'em. A shipwright by the name o' Lucky Peck said to them, 'Are you bound yet, boys?' They said, 'No, not yet, Mr. Peck.' So he said, 'Right! We'll bloody soon bind yuh!' They got hold of 'em, tied 'em together back to back, laid 'em on some larnchin' ways which were in the water and let the tide rise up round 'em. That scared the boys stiff, as you can imagine. Another thing the blokes used to do was git hold of a couple o' the apprentices at dinnertime (if they could catch 'em) and take 'em inta the big covered place if there wasn't a ship layin' there. Then they'd tie a rope round each of 'em, throw one end up over a couple o' the roof trusses (they were about ten or 12 foot apart) and hoist 'em up to about six foot orf the ground. After that they'd swing the boys apart and let 'em continually keep bumpin' each other till the momentum gradually ceased.

"Oh, there used to be some laughs on that yard! One o' the shipwrights, a chap named Jack Pitchers, would kid some o' the boys up to go out for a scull with him in the yard boat. Well, when they got out in the middle o' the water, he'd pull the plug out and start screamin' for help. He'd hold his hands up and shout, 'Help! Help! We're sinkin'!' And as soon as someone tried to put the plug back in, he'd kick their hand away. Eventually the boat would git back to the shore awash to the gunwales. Yeah, the boys would all be sittin' round the gunwale with their feet and legs in the water. You know, he wouldn't let 'em put the plug back in. And then they'd hafta wade ashore because the boat was too full o' water to pull up. Us boys used to take that boat sometimes and go and fight the apprentices from Colby's yard on the other side o' Lake Lothing. This would be at dinnertime. With the steelyards bein' in vogue, there was always plenty o' ammunition layin' about in the form o' plate washers and service nuts and bolts. We used to load the boat up wi' them and go orf to battle with the enemy boat in the middle o' the river. Yeah, we'd pelt each other wi' these nuts and bolts, and use oars. And, I can tell yuh, it isn't very pleasant gittin' a 16 foot oar on the napper! Oh, we used to fight like hell, we did. That was in fun more or less, but if you got a bit angry with each other that led to a real fight.

"While on the subject o' boats, Chambers had their own rowin' club. Yeah, when the war ended and the steelyard opened, there were various things started – like a football club, a darts club and a rowin' club. I was always in the rowin' club, even though I was only a featherweight, and we had two old ex-Naval whalers, the *Here We Are* and the *So Are We*. The timbers were pretty rotten on 'em, but we stiffened 'em up a bit and put a load o' pitch down in the bottom to keep the water out. We used to row against a Navy team in them. Yeah, the blokes orf the monitor, *H.M.S. Havelock*, which lay in the Hamilton Dock. There used to be five people rowin' in a whaler and then the cox'n on top o' them. I was even stroke for a time, so I cheated a bit. Yeah, I took my oar hoom, bored a hole down the shaft and filled it wi' lead, which helped me to balance better. See, we were all so small in our crew, where some o' the other boats were big. Colby's shipyard, for instance – their blokes were gret roasters and they used to beat us hollow. We used to row out round Pakefield Gat Buoy from the harbour and the stroke oar would hafta be balin' nearly all the time or we'd have sunk! Another course was up the River Waveney to Burgh Staithe and back. Yeah, and by the time we got back the water would be nearly up to the gunwale, and we'd hafta wade ashore.

"My apprenticeship should have been seven years, but the law was altered so that anybody who had served five years by the time he had attained the age o' 21 was released. Your time started from the day you began work. Yeah, so I began in the April o' 1916, but was actually bound apprentice in the September. I came out o' my time on my 21st birthday, August 31st, so I'd done six years and four months from when I'd started. When you came out o' your time, you maybe stood your workmates a round o' drinks. That all depended on circumstances. There weren't all that many ceremonial occasions on the yard – except on larnchins, when you'd praps have a bottle o' beer to give the boat a send-orf. When I started work, my rate o' pay for the first year was four shillins (20p) a week, and that went up a shillin' (5p) each year till it reached ten shillings (50p) in the seventh and last year.

"O' course, I earnt a lot more than that durin' the war years. I got the extra three shillins (15p) for goin' out to mark timber and then there were the war bonuses. I forget exactly what they were now, but they increased our wages considerably. You got time and a quarter or time and a half on overtime, dependin' on what was what, and you got double time on Sundays. We worked on Sundays quite a lot durin' the war, as I said earlier, puttin' down guns on standard drifters. Even after the war I earnt some good money. Yeah, before I was out o' my time we built two barges for Liverpool and I remember earnin' £7 one fortnight on them, a-plankin' the hulls up. See, you didn't git paid weekly when you were doin' that sort o' job; you got paid when the firm knew what time you'd taken. They gave yuh some money to be goin' on with, but not the full amount. See, a job like that, which might take a fortnight or three weeks, they couldn't work out your wages till the whole thing was done.

"I mean, say you were given 100 hours to do a job and you got it done in 86 – well, you'd earnt those other 14 hours in less time. Yeah, you got paid for the whole job, but you'd finished it in less time and could start another one, you see. That was the incentive – piecework. That was brought in durin' the war, but the firm didn't really like it because it can lend itself to frivolous workmanship. You know, it can become skimped work, in just the same way that some trainee work is. Trainees can't always see the reason why things are done in a certain way, whereas if you've ben apprenticed to a job you know why.

Trainee work came in durin' the Second World War, and though the trainees were usually all right they were brought in to fill a gap. That meant they didn't always do things the right way.

"When apprentices came out o' their time, at the time I'm talkin' about, they got 39 shillins (£1.95) a week. Exclusive of war bonuses, that is. Yeah, and my father would have been gittin' about 28 shillins (£1.40). All bonuses were drastically cut in one fell swoop after the war, and we didn't know how to feel for a time because that was a big reduction in wages. It was done in just one cut and you were right down. We did continue to work overtime, though, and I can remember a very funny incident that occurred one time when we were caulkin' a standard drifter's deck. There was one o' the apprentices who was a very cheeky boy and he was sittin' on the foredeck amongst the caulkers. Well, one o' the shipwrights, named Percy Jillings, asked him to shift and he wouldn't. He asked him more'n once, but the boy wouldn't move. Well, a lot o' boys came from poor families at that time and had to wear hand-me-downs. I've even known boys to come to work in their sisters' shoes, they were so poor. This boy was wearin' an extra long jacket on this particular day and it had a long bob tail that was flaked out behind him on the deck where he sat. Well, as I said, he wouldn't move when he was asked, so Percy Jillings just kept caulkin', jacket and all! Yeah, that jacket was caulked into two or three seams, so when the boy tried to git up he couldn't move. He had to wriggle out o' his jacket and there it was, caulked inta the seams! O' course, the jacket had to be cut orf at the deck; there was nothin' else for it. That boy always shifted up when he was asked to after that.

"As regards the actual hours we worked (the normal hours, I'm talkin' about), we used to start officially at six o' clock and work till eight. Then we had a half-hour for breakfast. We went through till one o' clock, took an hour orf for dinner, and then worked two till five in the afternoon. Yeah, and on Saturdays we went in from half-past eight till one. In the autumn the hours were reduced to quarter-past six and quarter to five, (this was through an agreement between the union and the management), and in the winter to half-past six and half-past four. Then, when spring came, that'd be back to quarter-past six and quarter to five and to six and five in the summer again. But even when the hours were shortened, you were still expected to do your complement o' work for the day. There was an allotted amount o' work to do per day and you used to do it in the short time just as well as you did in the longer one. I think the reason for that is this: in the cooler weather you were able to do more in a certain amount o' time than you could when that was warm. You tend to feel more lethargic in warm weather, don't you? See, and that was hard work. Shipwrightin' was really hard work, all of it.

"On Saturdays the blokes at Richards only worked till 12. Yeah, Richards were always ahead of everybody else in reducin' hours; though later on, o' course, the 47 hour week was brought in. That was agreed between the unions and the employers, but the employers wanted the breakfast half-hour cut out and the men to start work a half-hour later. Well, the shipwrights wanted to carry on as normal and they went on strike about it. This would be some time in the early 1920's, because I remember I was still an apprentice. Yeah, I was workin' down on the steelyard and I was the only one there. I was puttin' teak bridge rails on coasters and the foreman used to come down once every three or four days just to see how I was gittin' on. The strike lasted for about seven weeks altogether and, when it finished and the men went back to work, Richards gave all their shipwrights ten shillins (50p) each. That was a little gift to their employees, because there wasn't social security in them days. One man refused to take it; it was a matter o' principle, he said. I was in the Shipwrights and Ship Constructors' Union. It was quite strong at John Chambers and I joined it as soon as I started work. I used to pay thrippence (1½p) a week subs. and I even went to the meetins occasionally. When I first started work, there were no such things as canteens; you used to sit and eat your food wherever you fancied. And there were no proper toilets, either. After the war, though, things changed. Oh yeah, conditions improved. When the steelyard opened, a canteen with trestle tables in was put up and there were decent toilets built."

From 1922, up until the outbreak of war in 1939, much of Ted Frost's working life was spent at sea on vessels belonging to the Furness company. There were a couple of spells, though, when he returned to shipwrighting. The first came during the General Strike in 1926, when he spent three weeks in the Richards yard at Lowestoft caulking the prototype diesel drifter *Veracity* (LT 311) and then some time at John Chambers building a pilot boat. In 1935 he went to the Richards yard again for a period of about 18 months, working on the diesel trawlers *Willa* (LT 33) and *British Columbia* (GY 153). The 1930s also gave him the initial experience for his third career, civil engineering. Among the schemes he worked on were Southwold Harbour (1937) and Pakefield Sea Wall (1938). He was back in Richard's Yard during the war but afterwards worked for 21 years as a construction site foreman and clerk of works. He has never forgotten the allure of the sea and its craft, especially the grace of line which distinguished that most-loved of all fishing boats, the steam drifter.

Scottish drifters packed into Great Yarmouth harbour on a Sunday just before the First World War. They used to be packed in so tight you could walk on them from one side of the harbour to the other.

Lowestoft had a fish canning factory as early as 1870, started by the Maconochie brothers, local merchants. In the 1920s they built a new factory block, later acquired by the Co-operative Wholesale Society and seen here decorated for the Silver Jubilee of King George the Fifth. (Courtesy Jack Rose)

CHAPTER THIRTEEN

Triple Expansion

'Lord, thou hast made this world below the shadow of a dream
An', taught by time, I tak it so – exceptin' always steam.
From coupler-flange to spindle-guide I see they hand, O God –
Predestination in the stride o' yon connectin' rod.'
('McAndrew's Hymn' – Rudyard Kipling)

It took a long time, until almost the very end of the 19th century, for steam drifters to arrive on the scene. Steam was used to drive capstans on sailing drifters from about 1885 and this technology was dominated by the firm of Elliott & Garrood of Beccles. With the arrival of steam propulsion, however, a number of companies began to turn their attention to constructing compound surface-condensing units, followed in due course by more powerful triple-expansion engines. In Great Yarmouth two engine builders stood out – Burrell and Crabtree and they were practically next door to each other, beside the yard belonging to Fellows & Co. Ltd, perhaps the best-known of all the town's shipbuilders. Bert Stubbs (born 1903) served his apprenticeship as a marine fitter & turner with Crabtree Ltd. before proceeding to a career in the Merchant Navy.

"I don't know where I got my interest in steam from. I suppose I used to see the trains come into Gorleston station and notice the old road rollers, and I suppose I wanted to know what made the wheels go round. Anyway, I expressed a wish to be an engineer, so my father put me apprentice. It was a fairly difficult time to get an apprenticeship then because a lot o' the places were full up. It was wartime, you see, 1917, and I think a lot o' young fellers had gone into engineering to keep out o' the Army. It was a protected industry, you see, what with all the war work bein' done. And apart from that, it wasn't easy to get into Crabtree's in those days without p'raps having a brother or cousin or someone there, so you had a bit of influence. Well, we didn't have anything like that. My father paid a premium of sixty guineas for me and that was a lot o' money in them days, I can assure you.

"I was bound for five years and the wages stated on the indentures were three shillings (15p), five (25p), seven (35p), nine (45p) and 11 shillings (55p) a week. I got a bit more than that actually because we got paid war bonus, but that was what was on the indentures. I done about three weeks or a month to start with, just to see if I liked it or not, and then I actually started my apprenticeship about the 6th o' November, 1917. In them days, when you came out o' your time, they'd probably expect you to do about a year as an improver. Yeah, they considered that you were still not fully experienced, you see, and they'd probably pay you somethin' like 35 bob (£1.75) or £2 a week. As far as I can remember, the full wage when I came out o' my time was about £2.12.6d (£2.62½p). Unfortunately, I got stood off when I finished my apprenticeship because things had slackened right away. There just wasn't the work about. Things picked up a little in 1923 when some o' the drifters fitted out with seine-net winches and went fishin' the Dogger Bank, but generally speakin' the bottom fell right out o' everything. It was different before the war; they were building drifters and engines as fast as they could then. And the wartime itself was busy, o' course.

"There were about 12 to 14 apprentices in the engineer's shop when I was doing my time. When you finished, you were supposed to be a tradesman then, a fitter and turner. A fitter, turner and erector it says on the indentures, which is a bit of flowery talk really, I suppose, because you were just a fitter. In order to be anything better than that, you had to go and get some qualification certificates – things like the Board of Trade transport certificate or City and Guilds.

"One or two o' the apprentices at Crabtree's took Bennett College courses. They were done from Sheffield on a correspondence basis and they were very good things on marine engines. You paid about £6, I think, and you got four or five nice books as part o' the course. There used to be evening classes you could attend as well and a lot o' the boys used to go to them. They were voluntary and we attended the old Science School on South Quay, Yarmouth. Monday was machine construction and drawing, and Mr. Chamberlain who was in charge o' the drawing office took that. Wednesday was maths, taken by a teacher called Mr. Cornet, and Friday was applied mechanics. Oh, there used to be a good turnout. Us boys were pretty keen. See, a lot of us had the idea o' going to sea in the Merchant Service or something like that. As it happened, it was a bit of a job to get to sea in the middle 20s, but I did eventually manage it."

After finishing at Crabtree's, Bert Stubbs did a number of jobs before going into the Merchant Navy in 1929. Part of the time he spent as engineer on the Gorleston voluntary lifeboat, *Elizabeth Simpson*. This vessel was run independently of the official RNLI boats, being the responsibility of the Ranger Beach Company, one of those uniquely East Anglian freelance salvage co-operatives that were a feature of the coast in days gone by. He finished his career as a chief engineer with the Blue Star Company. Wearing a suit of white ducks was a far cry from those early days in Crabtree's engineering shop where the man's working life was shaped.

"The usual routine was for the new boys to start on a small shaping machine, which did small bearings and other parts o' the engine. It was a thing where the tool moved over the surface o' the metal and gave a nice smooth finish. Next to it was a big shaping machine, looked after by a Mr. Pratt, and it was his job to look after the new boys and show 'em what to do. We did about six months on the shaping machine, then we moved onto a lathe and done fairly simple turning jobs to start with. You know, makin' bottom-end bolts, top-end bolts, main bearing bolts and that sort o' thing. When we'd got a bit more experienced, we went onto screw cutting and boring out all the different bearings, and we were on that for about two to three years. That was the turning part o' the apprenticeship, you see. Finally, we were moved down onta the bench and there we done the fitting and erecting. We got jobs like bedding in and fitting bearings, doing link gear and tubing condensers. Then, when the engines were taken out to the ships, you went down to the quay with the fitters.

"One thing we had to do, o' course, was line the engine up with the propeller shaft. After that it was bolted down to the *sole-plate*. Previous to that we'd probably have been working on boring out the stern-tube when the ship was still on the yard. There was a proper travelling tool to do that, which was used by two men. It cut as it went round and it moved forward as well. Inside the tube itself were *lignum vitae* splines and the shaft ran on them. Oh yes, and they could be renewed if any wear took place. Another thing we done was make all the pipes for the boilers. They were *Scotch boilers*, o' course, and they used to be dropped into place by the sheer-legs as well. And before the ship was launched we'd probably done what were called *skin-fittings* – you know, the injections and dischargers on the ship's side. Then, if you were lucky, you eventually went out on the trials.

"They did all the designing o' the engines at Crabtree's, you know. Yes, it was done in the drawing office, where Mr. Chamberlain worked with his assistants, and then after the drawings were done the pattern-makers would make up all the various wooden patterns for the different parts. After that the patterns were taken into the foundry and moulded in sand or grit ready for the castings to be done. They'd be days and days in the foundry getting all the things ready and then all the different bits would come into the machine shop to be finished off. You know, measured and machined according to the dimensions on the drawings. We didn't do propeller shafts, they were a fairly big forging and got done somewhere else, but we did make the propellers themselves. With the engines, the fitters would lay the bed-plate first and then build the engine up from there. The small bearings (you know, for things like pump links and that) were usually made of brass, but the bigger ones were white metal. There was no forced lubrication on the main bearings. You just had oil-boxes and you kept them full so that the oil was siphoned down to where it was needed.

"There was a lot o' things done with a hammer and chisel in them days, where it was mechanically done with an electric motor later on. I mean, the fitters would cut holes through the deck or hull on steel ships with a round-nosed chisel when they were putting in valves or anything like that. I've seen keyways cut into spindles and cogs with a hammer and chisel. Oh yes, there was fair bit of hard work involved in a number o' things. I remember going with an old fitter by the name o' George Burgess to do a repair job on the old Yarmouth bridge. I'm talking now about the early 1920s. There was a tooth broken on the big gear wheel in the bridge lifting machinery and we went and put a new one in. That was all done by hand, with hammer and chisel and file. We dovetailed and bedded it in to make a nice fit and everything. It was a good piece o' work. But, there you are, Crabtree's had a very good name. There's no doubt about it.

"The biggest engine that I can remember being built was what was called a Triple Nine. I couldn't tell you exactly what the dimensions of it were, but it went into one o' the big naval tugs called the *St. Aristell.* There were a number of tugs named like that; the *St. Just* was another. They were built to last, them boats. I saw one out in Sydney, Australia, in about 1968. I think it actually was the *St. Aristell.* She'd been renamed, o' course, but there she was still going strong. I'll tell you another place where there used to be quite a bit o' shipbuilding going on as well – Selby, in Yorkshire. Cochrane's was the firm there and sometimes coasters they'd built would be towed down to Yarmouth to be engined at Crabtree's. I remember working on one, but I can't tell you the name of her now."

The Yorkshire port of Selby on the River Ouse built a considerable number of Yarmouth and Lowestoft steam drifters, especially in the golden days of the herring prior to 1914. The best working example of a Crabtree triple-expansion engine (it may be the only surviving one) is to be found in the steam drifter-trawler *Lydia Eva* (YH 89), which is at present part of the Maritime Trust's collection in St. Katharine's Dock, London. The vessel itself was built at King's Lynn in 1930, 13 years after Bert Stubbs had begun his engineering career.

"Yarmouth was quite a big naval base when I started work. There was submarines there and torpedo boats as well. Then there was the armed trawlers, o' course, and all that sort o' thing. Well, that meant there was plenty o' repair work, you see, apart from any new work what might come inta the yards. Or a ship might come in for a survey. There was all sorts o' Board of Trade surveys; coasters used to come in at regular intervals for them. I also went to work on a lot o' vessels that came in with engine trouble. After the war we even got foreign boats coming in, you know – small continental coasters. Some of 'em had what were called Bollinder engines in them; they were a sort o' diesel but with a hot bulb. That's right, you used to get a blowlamp and heat the bulb up to get the engine started. Crabtree's never built anything like that, but they did do repair work on them.

"With a *triple-expansion engine* you could sometimes run on two cylinders if the other one had broken down. It just depended which one was out of action, but sometimes you could make the steam get through. Yes, I can remember standing by a ship in the Atlantic which was trying to compound, as they called it. It was blowing a gale o' wind and she'd broken down. They tried hard to compound her, but they couldn't do it, and eventually we got a line across to her and towed her into The Azores. *Compound engines* are two cylinders and triples are three. Crabtree's might have made compounds, but the ones I can remember are the triples. The donkey pumps on those used to pump the bilges out and they also brought up water for the boiler and the deck hoses. When I was at sea, the average pressure on a Scotch boiler was about 200 pounds to the square inch, so 160 to 180 would be a reasonable figure for the earlier ones. I don't know how many revs the old drifters done, but I should imagine they went well over 100 when they were poofing round. Yes, 150 perhaps when they were going full ahead. But I'm more or less guessing now; I just can't remember.

"Once the engine and boiler were in a boat, she had a harbour trial. Extra moorings were put on and then the engine was run for the best part o' the day. Yes, they'd manoeuvre her up and down to see how she ran alongside the quay and they'd give her full speed ahead, but in such a way that the strain on the ropes or wires was taken up gradually. They'd give her a kick or two astern as well, just to make sure that everything was all right, and then later she'd be taken out on the proper sea trials. You had a measured mile on that, set between two points on the shore, and you ran the length of it to see what speed the boat would do. You set the compasses that day as well; yes, the compass people came specially aboard for that. And you'd maybe have a few drinks by way of a little celebration. I remember when I was on a ship at Cammell Laird's, later on in life, and the drink came aboard in a big box marked 'Medical Supplies'! I shall never forget that. I went on trials at Crabtree's mainly on tugs and coasters; I didn't work on fishing boats quite so much. We used to get steam up in the morning and go round doing last minute adjustments and things, then we'd take her out.

"When I first started at Crabtree's, the men were working till nine o' clock at night. Us apprentices didn't; we left off at half-past five. Our hours were from half-past six in the morning till half-past eight, and then from half-past eight till nine was breakfast. We started work again at nine and went through until one. Then we had the lunch hour from one o' clock until two. In the afternoon we went from two o' clock till half-past five and then knocked off. On Saturdays we finished at one and then went off to the football match. That's right. And you can imagine how we enjoyed a lay-in on the Sunday morning after being up for half-past six all during the week. The men who were working overtime went through till nine (see, things were very busy then) and they got time and a half, I think it was, with double time for Sundays. The old man, old Mr. Crabtree, used to keep an eye on things. Yes, he used to walk through the works every day. He was an upright, grey-haired old gentleman and he lived in that great big house at the top o' Gorleston High Street – you know, 'The Towers', where the Hewett trawling company's manager, Hervey George once lived.

"One thing about the firm was that everything ran very, very smooth. You never heard of what we get so often today – trouble over trivialities. I mean, if there was any complaint made, the matter was either rectified or accepted by the person who had made it. Yes, everything went pretty smoothly and there was a good atmosphere in the place. We never got holidays as such, only Christmas and Easter, but there used to be a works outing once a year in the summer. That was usually held on a Saturday and you'd all go out in the old brakes they had in those days. You'd go out to one o' the country pubs, where they'd have a lunch ready for you, and then the rest o' the day was spent drinking or whatever.

"I liked it at Crabtree's. There was a happy atmosphere in the place, and there was some very nice old-fashioned types among the men. The older blokes were always pullin' your leg about different things. I suppose with such long working hours in those days you needed something to cheer you up a bit. That's right. Yes, I mean, if you had a day off, or were a bit late for work in the mornin', you'd find your machine all decorated up or something. And another thing they done was nail the boys' dinner baskets to the bench or fill 'em up with old bolts and things. Then, when the hooter went and you made a rush to get the basket and be away, you couldn't shift it! I think there were initiation ceremonies as well, but I never saw anything o' that. I heard that they used to tie the apprentices on a ladder and cart 'em all round the shop. Yes, I heard about that, but I didn't see it.

"We used to clock in and out on a Bundy time-recorder. Yes, we all had our own key and a key number on the board, and if we weren't in at half-past six in the mornin' we could clock in for seven and lose half an hour's pay. If we weren't there by seven we had to wait until nine o' clock, which meant losin' a quarter, as they called it – a quarter-day, you see. There was one chap who worked on one o' the big planing machines (that was used to take a cut over the surface o' the big castings and smooth them off) and he was always bein' late for work. Yes, he'd lost no end o' quarters. One particular mornin' his table was empty (the machine was a big table thing, you see, what moved up and down), so the boys got one o' the long tool cupboards and laid it down on the table. Then they got a Union Jack from the office or somewhere (one what was used for trial trips) and put that over the coffin, like. After that they went round to some o' the cottages nearby and got some flowers out o' the gardens, made up a wreath and put that on top o' coffin as well. Now, this chap lived in Cobholm Island, quite near Breydon Water, so they made up a little rhyme for him. I can still remember that verse. It said: 'His deeds are done / His work is o'er / He resteth now on

Breydon shore / Not dead – sleeping!' Yes, I'll always remember that. And poor ol' Harry Chapman, the foreman, he used to stutter a bit, and when he saw all this he said, 'Y-y-y-you'll all f-f-f-finish up d-d-d-drivin' the sh-sh-sh-shitcart!'

"When the war ended there were big celebrations, o' course. Yes, they tied the hooter down for knocking-off time – tied it down and knocked off early. That was a steam thing, you see. I missed all that because I was off work with Spanish flu. Yes, I was laid up for about three weeks altogether. For sick pay I belonged to the Hearts of Oak Benefit Society. It was a friendly society like the Foresters and all those and I paid into it for years – just small weekly contributions, you know. See, there was no welfare state the same as we have now, so you had to sort o' prepare for a rainy day. The employers paid a health stamp for you as well and that was deducted from your wages. I know the apprentices at Fellows found out that too much was being stopped for the stamp and they passed the information on to us. We enquired about it and we were all called into the office and questioned about it by the secretary – you know, where we got the information from and all that. I don't think we were very popular over that, but the payment was adjusted. As regards trade unions, they had them at Crabtree's, but you weren't forced to belong to them. I can't remember what ones there were now, but I didn't belong to any. I only joined a union later on, when I got into the Merchant Navy.

"The General Strike in 1926 was a very big thing, o' course, but I can remember a coal strike in 1924 as well. My brother was skipper of a *seine-net* drifter called the *Kiama* (YH 766) and he went over to Holland to bunker coal at Ymuiden. I went over with him and then we went up to the Dogger Bank and worked a week before comin' home. I remember when the herrin' fishing was in full swing there used to be good prices for the catches over at Ymuiden, and the boats would go across there and sell them. Oh yes, that was done quite a lot. On the seine-netting my brother had an accident. Yes, he got wound round one o' the winches' drums and broke his collar bone and did other injuries to himself. They heaved the anchor up straight away and came home and landed him in the early hours o' the mornin'. He was taken to hospital there and then and he managed to get over it. The only thing was that he could never lift his arm much above shoulder level. He kept going skipper, though. Oh yes.

"I was seasick that time I went with him. I was right enough to watch the fishing, but I was seasick. Rolling around out there – oh dear, oh dear, what a life! The best part of it was when we were steaming home to Yarmouth again. Yeah, even the crew got in the wheelhouse then and sang at the tops o' their voices! My brother done all right at seine-netting, though. Oh yes, yes. The boat was owned by a Scotch army captain and he had his regimental colours painted on the funnel – purple and green halves, yeah. My brother was in several drifters in his time, but he certainly did all right on the seine-netting. What they did was drop a dan buoy, steam round and shoot the net, come back and pick up the dan, then haul both warps in together. As soon as the cod end came up and the catch was on deck, they'd let go and off they went again. It was hard work, but any sort o' fishing was. And those little boats – the size of 'em when you went down below! Those cabins, where the men all used to sleep and argue and talk! They were good sea ships, though – even if they were a bit let down as regards to maintenance."

The giant sheerlegs crane on the north side of Lowestoft inner harbour. In its day it was a prominent landmark seen well out to sea by homeward bound ships.

CHAPTER FOURTEEN

Railway Days

'In eighteen hundred and forty-six
I changed my trade from carrying bricks.
I changed my trade from carrying bricks
To work upon the railway.'
('Working On The Railway' – traditional)

The influence of railways as a factor in the expansion of the British fishing industry during the mid 19th century has long been recognised. Whether the tracks were built to improve the facilities of an existing harbour as at Great Yarmouth and Lowestoft, or were laid to create a completely new port as at Grimsby, the results were the same – rapid overland transport of catches to growing markets and faster essential supplies for the port itself. In the latter case that especially meant coal.

Steam power had revolutionised the British trawling fleets much earlier than the herring drifters, the first being built in the 1880s. Large amounts of coal were able to be brought by rail quickly and fairly cheaply, even to ports some distance from the coalfields. Both Great Yarmouth and Lowestoft are good examples of this, because their sailing smacks required coal for the capstan boilers just as much as those of the large fleets in Hull and Grimsby did. When steam engines came to the herring difters at the very end of the 19th century the resultant increase in catching capacity ensured that sailing vessels were soon replaced. Large coal depots sprang up near the railheads. With the new boom in fishing which came in the wake of steam drifters it was by rail that the large numbers of Scottish fisher girls and other itinerant workers arrived for the beginning of the autumn herring season and left at the end of it. Newham Timm (1899–1984) was station master at Yarmouth Vauxhall during the 1950s and 60s and he gives a good idea of the importance of rail transport in the declining years of the North Sea fishery.

"During the Second World War I was District Inspector, Cambridge, but stationed at Bury St. Edmunds. After the war I was promoted to Senior Inspector at Norwich and I was there for three years before being promoted again to Station Master at Yarmouth Vauxhall. I started in August 1950 and I was there until I retired in 1962. Yarmouth had three stations at the time I got the job – Beach, Vauxhall and Southtown – and they all dealt with their own traffic. The Beach was to North Norfolk, Spalding, Peterborough and The Midlands – and via them to Scotland, incidentally, for the fishing people. Vauxhall was capable of dealing with all over the country and Southtown was mostly to London. The station that I worked in originally at Vauxhall was the old one, built in 1844. When I came to Yarmouth, they were building new houses after the war and widening the roads. As a result of the bombing many of the old places were not reinstated; they were created into a fresh Yarmouth town plan. There was not a great deal of visible damage when I arrived in 1950. Things were generally working pretty well.

"The first fishing season of my experience started in October, 1950. The Scotch boats started coming down the river early in the month. By this time the best of the herring fishing years had passed, but there were up to 150 or more Scottish boats in port, plus the local ones as well. The Scottish boats never fished on a Sunday, you know, but the Englishmen all did. That year we had two trains of Scotch fisher girls come down to Vauxhall. That was the first time, I think, they'd gone there. Previous to that they'd always come down to The Beach. In due course, at the end o' the season, we sent the two train loads o' girls back to Scotland. While they were in Yarmouth they were all employed by particular merchants, who would come down to the station and book so many seats or coaches according to the number o' girls who'd got to go back. The trains left Vauxhall about six o' clock at night, following each other to Aberdeen. And as soon as the girls got on board, they turned on the primus stoves and started cooking their teas. Primus stoves in the corridors, aye! Fire risk and all that! And you had to be careful who you put together. There was a fellow called Campbell and he booked seats for so many girls, who had to be kept separate from the other clan altogether – Macdonalds, I think. Yes, you had to have one lot further along the train or else you got trouble. But they were a happy-go-lucky lot for all that.

"It was a good season for the fishing, 1950, and I think it might have been the last good one. The whole market couldn't absorb all the fish that were caught and there were hundreds and hundreds of tons surplus. I was asked to find wagons and get them to the processing plant on the Humber, where they were making meal of them for agricultural purposes. At that time we used to run through the streets along the quay and take the wagons right down to the fish wharf, where the herrins were tipped into the open wagons. Just loose! All the juice droppin' out all the way through the streets back to Vauxhall. Oh, I was working till 11 o' clock one night, clearing the market of all the unwanted fish. We must have moved 60 or 70 wagons that night. I got in touch with Norwich Control to send me more. All those wagons loaded up with loose herrins – a dreadful sight, really! And there were two or three days when we were sending 'em at a very fast rate indeed, as fast as we could get the wagons. It was a great shame really, but the home market just didn't want the herrins. Anyway, after a few days I received a telegram from the yard master at Hull, asking us to cease sending him any more herrins. He'd got over 400 wagons o' herrins in his goods sidings at that time, which the factory couldn't handle fast enough to process. And they were stinking – oh, completely rotten! Decomposing herrins – 400 wagons of them! 4,000 tons of them! And he asked me to stop sending.

"As I say, I think that was the last good year of Yarmouth fishin'. After we got that telegram, the herrins were beinning to work out so the whole market was able to absorb them. But they did build, after that season was over, a processing plant towards the end o' Yarmouth Pier. It was built, but it was hardly ever used because there was never any more herrin' in real bulk. It's been demolished long since and all took away. The Scottish vessels still continued to come down after 1950, but they decreased year by year. Instead of 150 boats or whatever on the river, it came down to 70, 60, and eventually there were only half-a-dozen or so that tried it. They only stopped for a few days, then went away altogether. The fish just weren't there. At one time in Yarmouth you could walk across the river from one side to the other on the boats. They were packed in that tight. It was amazing how they got out. It wasn't like that in 1950, though. Oh no, no, no. It was beginning to die out then. But for some reason they had a very good season that one year.

"After the herrin' disappeared from our waters about here, the merchants who dealt in them had to get them from somewhere else. Herrins were still being caught off the north o' Ireland and the north o' Scotland, so they came by train down to Yarmouth. Into Vauxhall. Yes, they came with the passenger traffic too! Every Saturday morning they arrived, just after 11 o' clock. One particular man got quite a lot o' herrin' that way and he used to be at the station with his lorry to meet 'em. The fish used to come down attached to the rear of a through-train from Peterborough. It was a holiday train and they were at the rear in a van, packed in ice. See, this was the end o' July and in August time, that I'm talkin' about. Oh, that wagon o' fish came down from the north for several weeks for this one man. Round about 1953 or 54, it would be. By the time I finished in 1962 there was no fish trade. There was no fish trade at all. The herrin' were gone then, or practically gone, and the Scotchmen had just about stopped comin' down. Oh, it was pathetic! Yes, yes, very sad – especially when you consider how big the fishin' used to be.

"We had fish trains carry the edible fish to the markets. There was a fish train every day from Southtown to London; I had a fish train every day from Vauxhall to The Midlands; and The Beach had a fish train to Peterborough and The North. Yes, we each sent a fish train away about three o' clock in the afternoon with all good edible fish for the markets. It was sent away packed in ice, but I can't tell you what the freightage charge per ton was because I wasn't in the goods department. Once the boxes o' fish had been delivered, the empty wagons were worked back by control in the normal services. The goods agent at each station ordered so many wagons daily for all his traffic (different kinds o' wagon for different kinds o' traffic) and there was a control at Norwich which used to see that he got them. He might order ten or more wagons a day for fish and they would be supplied. They were what we called common user, which meant they would circulate over a whole area. The wagons which Southtown had today might be up at Grimsby another day. Nor did the wagons that were used for fish stay on fish. Oh no. And another thing – the edible fish was carried in box wagons, whereas the fish going to the factory for making up into agricultural manure etc. was transported in open ones.

"We used to send a lot o' bloaters and kippers away, you know. Yes, they were sent to the ports for exporting. In the early days, well before 1950, a great quantity o' Scotch-cured herrins was sent to Russia. There were different kinds o' herrins – marinated, Scotch-cured, and other types too according to the treatment they'd received after being caught. I don't remember us handling any o' the Scotch barrels, but it's possible that we did. Kippers and bloaters went, as I said, and there was a tremendous postage trade in them from the holiday visitors buying boxes of 'em and sending 'em away to friends and relations. Yes, there was a shop in King Street doing nothing else but selling to the visitors boxes of kippers and bloaters packed as presents. There were thousands of 'em, going all over the country. We never handled any white fish, though. No, Lowestoft was the place for that; it was a Lowestoft activity. We had a lot o' salt come down from Cheshire and up that way, though – wagon and wagon loads of it – and that was for the curers, Sutton and people like that. It came down in closed wagons, whereas coal and stuff which didn't suffer from the weather was in open ones – though you could easily sheet them over, o' course.

"We put all the coal for the drifters down along the quay, as well as the salt required. The sidings ran down past the town hall to about as far as where Cluer's motor car place is. Two or three times a day we used to go right down that quay – yes, there were scores and scores o' wagons down there. Bessey & Palmer handled a lot o' the coal for the boats and they were agents for Trinity House as well. Their manager had his office down on the quay and they were obviously very, very good customers o' the railway – something that the manager was very quick to tell me when I first came to Vauxhall. The Trinity House vessel used to take a lot o' coal. She was called the *Warden* and it was her job to look after all the lightships and buoys between the Humber and the Thames. When she came into port periodically to re-stock her bunkers, it was a sight I should like you to have seen. A line o' men, with baskets on their backs, used to empty the railway wagons and walk along a plank to tip the coal down into the ship. It was like watching a South African labour gang.

"And another thing, while we're on the subject o' coal. The power station at Yarmouth [closed down in 1985] runs on oil, doesn't it? – well, there was a time when it was going to be a coal-fired one. Yes, the coal was going to come into Vauxhall and I had to produce plans and give a lot o' consideration to it. I'd got to carry all this coal right along the quay and back it through the power station gates into a large, walled, coal-storage place. You know the big wall round the power station? – well, that's what it was intended for originally, to hold the coal. In the end it was never used for anything very much, because the place was fired on oil. It came up on tankers from London. It probably still does. Yes, they used to lay up against the quay and pump the stuff right into those big round storage tanks you see there."

"Although I was station master at Vauxhall, there were times when I supervised Southtown as well – holiday periods when the station master was away, or when he was off sick. There was a fish train running from Southtown at the time I took those duties on, and that was when fish trains were on the way out. No real trade, you see. Well, I could see that such a train wasn't justified, so I cancelled it. I wasn't very popular with the railwaymen (jobs disappearin', you see), but it just wasn't economic; there wasn't the fish to go. When British Rail wanted to close Southtown Station, there was one Yarmouth councillor who said, 'Whatever shall we do? How shall we deal with the goods traffic which Southtown is handling at present?' Southtown wasn't handling any goods traffic! Road traffic was taking everything, you see, but people outside o' the railway industry just didn't know.

"It made a tremendous difference right from the very beginning, road transport. About 1920 the government sold off all the surplus wartime lorries and any Tom, Dick or Harry could go and buy one. This is true. And this was the genesis of road transport, at the end o' the 1914 War. And it was the law that all railway freightage rates were public. Yes, they had to be public and made known. So Bill Smith, we'll say, goes and buys his lorry for £30 or whatever and goes to his local railway station. This is true. I know, because it happened to me. Yes, he goes to the station and he says, 'What's your rate per ton for carrying sand from A to B for such-and-such a firm?' And you had to tell him! It was the law. 'Oh, 25 shillings,' you'd say. See, you had to tell him. Well, he'd go off to the consigner then and offer to carry the stuff for 15 shillings. Now, there were hundreds and hundreds of Bill Smiths with their lorries, all over the country, and that was the beginnin' o' road transport as we know it today. That's precisely how it all started.

"After a time all these operators joined themselves together and formed the Road Transport Federation. Oh, they realised that they were on a good thing and that the railways couldn't do anything about it. They had their voice in Parliament too. Oh, definitely. I could quote you the names and addresses of the men who started it all. Their power was in their own hands and we were aware that we couldn't really compete. I foresaw the end o' rail transport as the only big way of conveying goods as early as 1925. Yes, that's when all these chaps with lorries were going to the stations, enquiring about our rates, and then going straight to the person who was sending and underbidding us. And that's how you see history bein' made. You can't stop progress. Later on the motor car and the coach began to take away passenger traffic as well, but that wasn't as obvious at first as the government selling off all those surplus lorries.

"During my time in Yarmouth, o' course, the Beach station closed down. That was in 1959. When I first came to Vauxhall, the Beach was still handling a lot of holiday traffic from The Midlands and The North, but the decision was taken to close down the old Midland & Great Northern lines. Well, the question arose then as to which station was to survive in Yarmouth out o' Beach and Vauxhall. It was all a matter of which would be best for railway purposes and best for the public. As things stood, Vauxhall was the one. In fact, it was the best one of all three Yarmouth stations because it could do everything that the other two could do – whereas they couldn't do everything that it could. At least, not very easily. In the end, Southtown closed as well, but that wasn't till several years after I'd retired. I saw it coming, though. Oh yes, it was fairly plain to see with things the way they were. Anway, I argued strongly for closing the Beach and keeping Vauxhall, and in the end it was my argument which won the day.

"Once the decision had been taken to close The Beach, I had to draw up plans for receiving its holiday traffic at Vauxhall the following summer. All the staff at the Beach eventually left, except for one man who we left in the signal box. He was there to alter the points for the engineer's train, which needed to move round as it dismantled the tracks. They started lifting the tracks very soon after the station closed – very soon indeed. They started to take it to pieces within a few weeks. There was a physical connection by rail through the streets of Yarmouth between The Beach and Vauxhall, but all that colossal load o' gear which had been dismantled couldn't be taken out that way. So what they did was work it away to Norwich through Ormesby and Potter Heigham. In the end it all got too much for this man in the signal box. He'd been at Beach Station for many years and he was a very loyal M&GN servant. Well, each day he found more and more of his beloved railway being packed up on trucks and going away. It just got too much for him and he came to me one day at Vauxhall with his keys and said, 'No more. I shall not be there tomorrow.' There were tears in his eyes as he spoke and he didn't come back any more. He finished. He didn't live too long afterwards either – only three months or so – because he was absolutely broken up.

"Those men felt it, you know. It's true. They were loyal – loyal to the core to the railway and the steam engines of their day. The diesel and the electric trains of today don't seem to generate that spirit. Nor do the advance of time and the changes in labour relations. It all seems to be lost. A lot of it was to do with the engines, I think. See, a steam engine was an individual; a diesel or an electric one is not. It's purely a machine, whereas with a steam engine every one was different. Yes, that is true – every steam engine was different. One would make light of a heavy load; another one would not be a very good steamer, would not pull very well at all. Every one was different and it had an effect on the men. It helped to breed this tremendous loyalty and pride."

Those two Yarmouth stations which served the once thriving fishing industry and brought the thousands of holidaymakers whose sojourn by the sea must have been made more colourful by it, have long since been altered beyond recognition. All that remains now as a reminder of the part they played is a slatted platform seat from Yarmouth Southtown which has found a resting place far away in the foyer of the National Railway Museum at York.

Scottish fisher girls and coopers enjoying a bit of leisure time in Yarmouth early on in the 20th century. When they were not working the Scottish girls spent most of their time knitting, even as they went along when out for a walk.

CONCLUSION

'I'll sing you a song o' the fish o' the sea.
Way down Rio.
I'll sing you a song o' the fish o' the sea
And we're bound for the Rio Grande.'
('Way Down Rio' – old shanty)

Just before the First World War there were 600 steam drifters registered in Lowestoft and Great Yarmouth alone and the total number of British fishermen was over 100,000. Not only has the industry much diminished, but the pattern of operations so familiar to the people who have told their story in these pages has changed too.

As we have seen, fishing had always been an industry of movement and migration for those involved in it. This has become much less the case since the war, where the pattern has been increasingly for boats to work from their home ports no matter what the distances to the fishing grounds are. Traditional voyages have come to an end as falling catch-rates have made them no longer worthwhile and as relatively cheap diesel fuel made it easier to work longer trips than was possible in the days of steam and bunkered coal. Since the mid 1970s fishing has undergone considerable retraction in terms of the numbers of men and boats involved, owing to a combination of factors. The closure of Icelandic waters to British trawlers in 1976 effectively finished off Fleetwood and Hull as distant-water ports, while the steep rises in oil prices throughout the 70s made it increasingly difficult for vessels to make a profit. Then there is the effect of the E.E.C. 'common pond' policy, to say nothing of the arrival of East European trawling fleets with their accompanying factory ships.

This has naturally resulted in a marked decrease in the total of shore personnel. The steady fall in the number of boats working and dwindling catches have had a large part to play in causing this, but one has also to consider the effect of the disappearance of drift-netting as a method of fishing (which was itself partly the result of the herring being overfished) and of the traditional ways of processing herrings in bulk. Compared with farming as it is now conducted, fishing remains a labour-intensive industry – but only where boats continue to work. If more of them could be got to sea, then the numbers of people employed would rise. How to achieve the increase is the question, and there is no easy answer. Fuel subsidies might result in more vessels putting out, but they would only provide a temporary boom. A longer term solution probably lies in developing new markets for the catches and perhaps in reviving old ones. The major food-processing companies could play a large part here, but until they diversify from the fish-finger concept and invest in new lines (and that investment includes convincing the customer of the desirability of such products!) sales will probably remain as they are. There are more species swimming around in the sea than just cod, haddock and plaice! Many of them are just as tasty, but the public palate needs to be convinced.

Two steam drifters in dry dock at Fellow's yard in Great Yarmouth in the 1930's. With her stern to the camera is the *Wydale* YH105.

GLOSSARY

Adze wood-shaping tool, with a curved axe-like blade set at right-angles to the handle.

Arles money paid in advance to Scottish gutting-girls by their employers as an acknowledgement of each party's contractual obligations.

Auger tool for boring holes in wood, rather like a large drill bit with a wooden handle set at right-angles to the end of the shank.

Baulks wooden bars set with regularly spaced metal hooks on which split herrings were impaled for kippering.

Beam trawl trawl net with its mouth kept open by a wooden spar.

Beating chamber net-store.

Beating knife small shutknife used by beatsters to split the knots on meshes.

Beatsters women who mended drift nets.

Bed-plate heavy cast-iron base of a marine engine.

Bicarb bicarbonate of soda.

Bilge maximum point of curve on a barrel.

Black-noses term used of herrings caught during November on the East Anglian home voyage.

Blade device for holding cotton skeins prior to loading beating needles.

Bloaters herrings lightly salted and smoked with the gut in.

Bogie low four-wheeled trolley.

Braiding making trawl nets.

Brakes carriages or wagonettes drawn by horses.

Brisling young herrings or sprats canned in brine.

Broads freshwater lakes of shallow depth in Norfolk and Suffolk, caused by the flooding of medieval peat diggings.

Brotches lengths of split hazel used to hold roof thatch in place.

Bucklings herrings smoked very hot so as to be partly cooked.

Bulking filling a barrel of pickled herrings improperly, but with the ends packed correctly.

Caulk to make a wooden ship's seams watertight by packing them with oakum.

Chase up to force up the price of a commodity at auction.

Chuck/chuck up to reject a catch of herrings after auction by claiming that the fish did not conform to the quality of the sample.

Coalie coalfish or saithe.

Cob herrings East Anglian October herrings.
Cod's chaps large rents in the meshes of a drift net.
Cod end bag at the end of a trawl net, which holds the fish.
Compound engine steam engine with two cylinders.
Condenser part of a steam engine which converts exhausted steam back into water.
Cooper man who makes barrels
Cran measure of 37½ Imperial gallons; 28 stones of herring by weight.
Creel basket for carrying fish.
Crew team of three gutting-girls.
Crofters small farmers in the Highlands of Scotland.
Culch East Anglian dialect word for dross or refuse.
Dan marker buoy used in trawling.
Day-book ledger in which a fish salesman's daily transactions were recorded.
Denes area of sandy heath or wasteland near the sea.
Dennies rejected cans in food processing.
Diet hours Scottish term for mealtimes during the working day.
Donkey part of a steam engine which worked the pumps.
Drifter boat that fished for herring or mackerel using drift-net gear.
Drifter-Trawler steam or motor vessel which drifted or trawled according to season.
Farlane large trough into which herrings were put ready for gutting.
Firkin quarter-sized barrel.
Fish-house smokehouse.
Fixing the contract of employment made between Scotch curers and their workers.
Flagging iron tool used to force barrel staves apart.
Flit-boat converted Scottish sailing drifter, with motor added, which conveyed coal and other commodities around the Shetland Isles.
Freshers merchants who traded in fresh herrings, or the boats which carried such cargoes abroad.
Fule an East Anglian variant of fool.
Fulls mature herrings which contain milt or roe.
Garden lint herring nets too badly damaged for fishing.
Gat East Anglian word for an opening in sandbanks through which ships could make safe passage.
Gip/gypy to gut herrings.
Golden herrings fish salted and then smoked for up to about a fortnight. A lighter cure than the red herrings.
Guarding meshes the heavier, reinforcing meshes around the edges of a drift net.

Gunwale	upper edge of a boat's side.
Ham	East Anglian word for a saltwater inlet and the marsh surrounding it.
Hawseman	man below mate on a steam drifter.
Heading	hemp cords on the side of a drift net.
Home fishing	East Anglian autumn herring season, pronounced 'hoom'.
Hot-bulb engine	type of internal combustion engine fuelled by paraffin.
Improver	term used of a worker who has finished an apprenticeship but has not achieved full status.
Inshore boats	fishing vessels which work just a few miles from land.
Journeyman	artisan who has completed his apprenticeship.
Jumbos	large fish of any kind, but particularly cod and haddock.
Kell/kill	kiln.
Keyway	slot cut into metal for the insertion of a component.
Kipper	herring that is split, salted and smoked.
Kit	wooden cask, open at one end, for the conveyance of herrings.
Kite	device used in sweeping mines.
Klondyke	to pack herrings in salt and ice in large wooden cases.
Klondyke trade	the exporting to Germany of herrings treated in the way described above.
Knobbing machine	device that decapitated the gutted herrings.
Larnchin'	East Anglian variant of launching.
Latchet	the tub gurnard.
Lignum vitae	very dense West Indian hardwood.
Longlining	catching bottom feeding fish with lines fitted with long series of baited hooks.
Longshore boats	small craft which fish close in to land.
Maatjes	Dutch term for medium-sized herrings without milt or roe in them.
Maise	eggs of the female herring. Hard roe.
Mands	wicker baskets for handling herrings and sprats.
Margarines	boxes containing three stones weight of herring.
Mashes	meshes.
Matties	gutted herrings of not less than nine inches in length.
Matfulls	herrings full of milt or roe which are not less than nine and a quarter inches long.
Milt	male herring's spawn. Soft roe.
Monitor	shallow-draught vessel carrying heavy guns.
Monkey island	lookout platform on top of an armed fishing boat's wheelhouse.
Monks	angler fish.
Needle	tool used by beatsters and braiders to make and mend fishing nets.

Net a boat	term used when a person other than the boatowner financed the purchase of a drifter's fishing gear.
Net-store	building where fishing gear was serviced and stored.
Nightman	fisherman who stepped in at short notice to deputise for another.
Norsels	lengths of twine which joined the meshes of a drift net to the netrope and which retained the corks in position.
Ossels	norsels.
Otter trawl	trawl net that has its mouth kept open by large wooden or metal doors.
Overdays	herrings caught the previous day.
Painted ladies	kippers which have been dyed to achieve a high colour.
Pamments	floor bricks, often square in shape.
Peck	Imperial capacity measure of two gallons.
Pickle	brine for curing herrings.
Pickling plot	area of land where herrings were given the Scotch cure treatment.
Pieces	Scottish term for fragments of food, especially cake and meat.
Piecework	system where people are paid for what they actually produce, not by an hourly rate.
Pigeon-feed	to sprinkle fish very lightly with salt.
Pining	pickling process involved in Scotch cure whereby the brine and herring juices mix together over a period of ten days.
Plank	wooden bench on which a basketmaker sits to work.
Pooling	post-war system for stabilising and controlling herring prices.
Premium	down-payment made to an employer for an apprentice starting work.
Prick on	fix split herrings to baulks prior to smoking them for kippers.
Prime fish	halibut, sole, turbot and brill – the more valuable species.
Pull down	clean drift nets after a catch of fish.
Purse seine	large bag-shaped net which is drawn round a shoal of fish.
Quarter-hoops	bands around a barrel either side of the middle one.
Quarters	area of a barrel between the end and the middle. Also, the after part of a vessel where the sides of the hull join the stern.
Retainer	Small payment made to employees during a close-season period to ensure their services when required.
Retorts	kilns for the cooking of tinned foods.
Ring net	type of drift net worked so as to enclose a shoal of herrings.
Ring netters	boats or fishermen using the above method.
Ripper	fishing line worked by hand and having its hooks attached to a lead weight.
Roaring/rousing shovel	wooden shovel used for salting or moving fish.
Roker	thornyback ray, also applied to other members of the ray family.

Roll mops strips of raw herring pickled in vinegar and other preservatives.
Rough packs herrings that were salted and packed loosely into kits.
Roused term used of herrings salted down on the ground.
Rows roes.
Runties East Anglian term for Scottish sailing drifters.
Scotch boiler boiler where the heat passes through tubes to raise the temperature of the surrounding water.
Scotch net cotton drift net.
Scran inferior or undersized herrings.
Sea-sticking term used for the initial filling and stacking upright of Scotch cure barrels.
Seed herrings very small, immature herrings.
Seine-netting stationary trawling, where the boat is anchored after the net has been shot and then hauling commences.
Selecting sorting out gutted herrings into the various sizes required for Scotch curing.
Selections herrings as sorted to above requirements.
Sheer upwards sweep of a boat's decks towards the bows.
Sheer-legs crane lifting apparatus of two main support poles.
Ship's husband man in charge of a fishing boat's crewing arrangements.
Shot quantity of herring caught in any one attempt.
Shruff woodshavings.
Sides top and bottom of a drift net.
Silver herrings fish that were salted and smoked for three or four days to a week.
Skin-fittings outlet and inlet pipes in a boat's hull.
Slip to put a vessel onto a slipway for inspection or repair. Also, the term used for a small sole.
Smack in the East Anglian sense, a ketch-rigged sailing trawler.
Sole-plate bedding in a vessel's engine-room onto which the engine itself was bolted.
Spents herrings that have shot their roes.
Split to cut herrings the particular way needed for kippering.
Spoilts damaged drift nets.
Spunyarn rope strands twisted together to make line for use in rigging.
Staithe inland wharf or harbour along a river-bank.
Standard drifter/trawler boat built to Admiralty specification during and just after the First World War.
Staves lengths of wood used in making barrels.
Stern-tube liner through which the propeller's tail-end shaft runs.
Stiffen reinforce the hull of a boat, or to build it stronger than in previous models.
Stocker bait/stockie money paid to trawlermen on top of their wages, made from

	the sale of small fish and uncommercial species.
Stone	14 pounds weight (about 6.5 kilos).
Stubs	trees or shrubs that have been cut off above ground level in order to stimulate growth – taller than a coppice stool.
Swill	Yarmouth wicker herring basket holding two-thirds of a cran.
Taffrail	rail around the after-deck of a boat.
Take off	term used for the movement of herring shoals from one area to another.
Tally	slip of paper with a fish merchant's name printed on it, used to denote purchase and ownership of catches.
Tan	preserve drift nets by boiling them in cutch.
Tins	aluminium herring boxes.
Triple expansion engine	steam engine with three cylinders.
Trunks	large wooden or metal fish boxes.
Turnings	woodshavings.
Tusks	torsks, fish of the cod family.
Vats	large under-floor tanks used to steep herrings in brine.
Voyage	total span of a fishing season in a particular area, not just one trip.
Wands	lengths of willow or osier used for weaving wicker articles.
Warps	hawsers or cables.
Water-tube boiler	boiler where the water is in tubes and the heat surrounds them. Quicker to raise steam than a Scotch boiler.
Ways	wooden or metal skids over which a boat is brought down to the water.
Went through	went bankrupt.
Whaler	heavy, clinker-built rowing boat – often with a pointed stern.
Wherry	shallow-draught freshwater barge, with large middle hold-section.
White fish	trawlfish.
White metal	soft alloy used to line engine bearings at one time.
Wings	parts of a trawl net nearest the otter doors.
Wrongs	branches of oak trees selected for their natural curve and used in constructing the hulls of wooden ships.

BIBLIOGRAPHY

Butcher, David *The Driftermen* (Tops'l Books 1979).
Butcher, David *The Trawlermen* (Tops'l Books 1980).
Butcher, David *Living From The Sea* (Tops'l Books 1982).
Butcher, David *The Cliffhanger* (East Anglian Resources Organisation 1983).
Cherry, P. & Westgate, T. *The Roaring Boys of Suffolk* (Brett Valley Publishing 1970).
Davis, F. M. *An Account Of The Fishing Gear Of England & Wales* (HMSO 1923).
Dyson, John *Business In Great Waters* (Angus & Robertson 1977).
Evans, George Ewart *The Days That We Have Seen* (Faber 1975).
Elliott, Colin *Sailing Fishermen In Old Photographs* (Tops'l Books 1978).
Elliott, Colin *Steam Fishermen In Old Photographs* (Tops'l Books 1979).
Festing, Sally *Fishermen* (David & Charles 1977).
Frost, E. J. *From Tree To Sea* (Terence Dalton 1985).
Gray, Malcolm *The Fishing Industries of Scotland* (Oxford University Press 1978).
Hedges, A. C. C. *Yarmouth Is An Antient Town* (Great Yarmouth Council 1959).
Hodgson, W. C. *The Herring And Its Fishery* (Routledge Kegan Paul 1957).
Joby, R. S. *Forgotten Railways: East Anglia* (David & Charles 1977).
March, Edgar *Sailing Drifters* (Percival Marshall 1952, reprinted David & Charles 1969).
March, Edgar *Sailing Trawlers* (Percival Marshall 1953, reprinted David & Charles 1970).
Malster, Robert *Lowestoft, East Coast Port* (Terence Dalton 1982).
Nall, J. G. *An Etymological and Comparative Glossary of the Dialect and Provincialisms of East Anglia* (Longmans, Green 1866).
Palmer, C. J. *The Perlustration of Great Yarmouth* (George Nall 1872–5).
Richards, L. E. *Eighty Years of Shipbuilding* (Richard Ironworks 1956).
Rose, Jack *Jack Rose's Lowestoft* (Panda Books 1981).
Rose, Jack *Jack Rose's Lowestoft Album* (Panda Books 1983).
Stibbons, Peter *Crabs and Shannocks* (Poppyland Publishing 1983).
Thompson, Paul *Living The Fishing* (Routledge Kegan Paul 1983).
Wren, Wilfred *Ports of the Eastern Counties* (Terence Dalton 1976).
The East Anglian, Vols 3 & 4 (Samual Tymms 1869).
Victoria County History of Norfolk (Archibald Constable 1901).
Victoria County History of Suffolk (Archibald Constable 1907).

SALE OF HERRINGS AT YARMOUTH.

A HULL TRAWLER.

Back cover picture:
Piles of swills awaiting use at Yarmouth just after the turn of the century. Swills were a design peculiar to Great Yarmouth and had a bar across the middle by which they were lifted.